SCHAUM'S™
EASY OUTLINES

Writing and Grammar

Online Diagnostic Test

Go to **Schaums.com** to launch the Schaum's Diagnostic Test.

This convenient application provides a 30-question test that will pinpoint areas of strength and weakness to help you focus your study. Questions cover all aspects of English writing and grammar covered by this book. With a question-bank that rotates daily, the Schaum's Online Test also allows you to check your progress and readiness for final exams.

Other titles featured in Schaum's Online Diagnostic Test:

Schaum's Easy Outlines: Spanish, 2nd Edition
Schaum's Easy Outlines: French, 2nd Edition
Schaum's Easy Outlines: German, 2nd Edition
Schaum's Easy Outlines: Italian, 2nd Edition
Schaum's Easy Outlines: Calculus, 2nd Edition
Schaum's Easy Outlines: Geometry, 2nd Edition
Schaum's Easy Outlines: Statistics, 2nd Edition
Schaum's Easy Outlines: College Algebra, 2nd Edition
Schaum's Easy Outlines: Biology, 2nd Edition
Schaum's Easy Outlines: Human Anatomy and Physiology, 2nd Edition
Schaum's Easy Outlines: Beginning Chemistry, 2nd Edition
Schaum's Easy Outlines: Organic Chemistry, 2nd Edition
Schaum's Easy Outlines: College Chemistry, 2nd Edition

Writing and Grammar

Second Edition

William C. Spruiell
Dorothy E. Zemach

New York Chicago San Francisco Lisbon London Madrid Mexico City
Milan New Delhi San Juan Seoul Singapore Sydney Toronto

The **McGraw·Hill** Companies

1 2 3 4 5 6 7 8 9 10 11 12 13 14 15   DOC/DOC   1 9 8 7 6 5 4 3 2 1

ISBN   978-0-07-176057-7
MHID   0-07-176057-1

Library of Congress Cataloging-in-Publication Data

Spruiell, William C.
    Schaums easy outline of writing and grammar / William C. Spruiell, Dorothy E. Zemach. — 2nd ed.
        p.   cm. — (Schaum's easy outline)
        Includes index.
        ISBN 0-07-176057-1 (alk. paper)
        1. English language—Rhetoric—Outlines, syllabi, etc.   2. English language—Grammar—Outlines, syllabi, etc.   3. Report writing—Outlines, syllabi, etc.
    I. Zemach, Dorothy E.   II. Title.   III. Title: Easy outline of writing and grammar.

    PE1408.S666   2010
    808'.042—dc22   2010039824

McGraw-Hill books are available at special quantity discounts to use as premiums and sales promotions or for use in corporate training programs. To contact a representative, please e-mail us at bulksales@mcgraw-hill.com.

This book is printed on acid-free paper.

Contents

Chapter 1
TARGETING
YOUR WRITING

Writing toward a Goal

Good writing must be aimed at a target. Whether you are writing a grocery list or a novel, you should write for a purpose and to achieve a specific goal or set of goals.

You can accomplish your goals if you aim your writing accurately at your readers. Keep your target audience in mind and constantly ask yourself if what you are doing will affect that audience in the ways you want it to.

If you are taking a composition class, you might think of your goal as "passing this course" or "making the professor happy," but in reality, the instructor is looking for evidence that you can adjust your writing to meet the kinds of goals you will encounter in real life as well as in school.

These goals can vary greatly, and different kinds of goals require different kinds of writing. Approach any kind of writing task by asking yourself two basic questions:

- What is my purpose?
- Who is my audience?

Your writing will improve if you keep your answers to these questions in mind as you write.

Purpose

If the only thing you think about as you write is whether or not your paper will get you a particular grade, you will probably find that the paper does *not* get you that grade. Instead, think about the kinds of goals your writing assignment might be designed to fulfill.

What if, for example, you were asked to write about a bank robbery. On the one hand you could write a fictional description as part of a novel or a short story. On the other hand, you could write it as part of a police report.

In both cases, you would want readers to have a clear mental picture of the people involved, their actions, and the order of events. You would use specific kinds of language (e.g. adjectives like "bright blue" to describe a clerk's jacket) to help the reader get a better mental image.

For the fiction version, you would be concerned with making the description as interesting as possible, since fiction writers have to hold an audience as part of their job. You might use colorful or deliberately unusual descriptions and describe the sounds of the robbery in vivid detail.

For the police report, however, making the description interesting would be much less important than making it absolutely accurate. You would probably avoid descriptions that are too colorful (the point is that a police report should *not* be fiction!) but be precise about the order in which the actions occurred.

Just as you have to decide your purpose in writing, you have to decide who your **audience** is. Even if you are convinced that your audience is just your English teacher, you should keep in mind that he or she represents a college-educated audience.

Most writing is targeted toward groups, and you need to know what groups you are

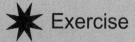 Exercise

What purposes might the following kinds of writing fulfill?

- A complaint letter to a business
- A short paper about the Spanish-American war
- A technical manual for a piece of industrial equipment

dealing with to write well. Whenever possible, you need to identify characteristics that all of your audience members share and other characteristics that may vary from one reader to another.

Therefore, a journalist *can* assume that his or her readers can read English written at a basic educational level and that those readers will have little difficulty with cultural references that are part of shared culture. The journalist *cannot*, however, assume that the readers are all male, have the same religious background, or hold the same political beliefs.

Whenever you write, you create an **image** of yourself as a writer. Therefore, once you have identified your purpose and target audience, you need to consider how to create the image you want.

The kind of language you use is a very important part of this image. Nonfiction writing, which includes journalism and business writing as well as research papers, essays, and school themes, customarily uses *Standard Written English*—a dialect of English that exists only in written form. *Spoken* English typically uses a slightly different set of rules and varies from place to place.

Another important element in your writing is the kind of emotion you project. For some purposes, and with some audiences, you will want your writing to seem highly emotional (for example, a description of the death of a loved one). In other cases, sounding strongly emotional will project the wrong image.

Writers use the term *tone* to describe the emotional characteristics the author projects, and setting the right tone is vital in any kind of writing. The most common problem inexperienced writers encounter with tone is being overly emotional in academic writing that is intended to explain or persuade. In this kind of writing, you want to seem interested

 **Note!**

Because Standard Written English is taught in schools and is no one's first language, it is associated with being educated. Most audiences expect that kind of language in writing.

and open-minded, but logical; you do *not* want to sound as if you are jumping up and down in anger or excitement.

To set the right tone in an academic paper you must also ensure that you create an image of yourself as a person who carefully considers both sides of an argument.

In fact, being careful is one of the most valuable traits you can project in an academic paper. Being careful also involves letting your audience know that the information you are including comes from reputable sources. You want to be trustworthy, and your audience will trust you more if they know that you have been careful about finding sources of information.

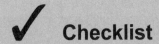 **Checklist**

When Writing Academic Papers:

- DO use Standard Written English.
- DO consider both sides of every argument.
- DO provide your sources of information when relevant.
- DO NOT sound as if you are extremely angry or extremely happy—try to sound calm and reasonable.

Your audience will approach your writing with certain expectations based on its prior knowledge and beliefs.

We expect scholars, for example, to sound educated, informed, and careful. People reading newspapers, on the other hand, expect yet another kind of writing style and approach.

You should also consider how much prior knowledge your audience has. As a writer, you cannot assume that your audience knows everything that you do. If you are writing a paper about the 1999 World Series, for example, ask yourself how many of your readers will know the baseball terms and players' names.

If you think some of your readers will lack the information necessary to understand your writing, it is your job to provide it.

At the same time, it is just as important not to explain points that the audience is already familiar with. If you use three sentences in a geography paper to explain to the professor where the North Pole is, he or she will probably think you are padding your paper. Again, the key is to target your purpose and your audience.

Chapter 2
THE WRITING PROCESS

Writing as a Process

There is a common belief that good writing is just a matter of inspiration—that it happens to some people and not others and that effort or learning has little to do with it. According to this belief, talented authors have some mysterious ability that lets them sit down with a pencil or computer and churn out pages of polished text.

Professional writers, however, know that this is false—a good final product is the result of a great deal of planning and work. The myth about inspiration is not just wrong, it is dangerous, since people who believe it think that if they *cannot* write an excellent piece of text at one sitting, they are incapable of good writing.

Writing is a craft, and like any other craft it involves learning skills and how to apply them. Professional writers vary enormously in the ways they approach the writing task, but they all approach it as a *process*, an activity that moves in stages and that takes time to complete.

Stages of Writing

The following diagram (see Figure 2-1) and discussion explain some of the common stages involved in any writing task. Writing involves steps that can, and often are, repeated. Writers frequently go back over their work, redoing portions to bring the whole closer to what they want (thus, many of the stages represented by boxes in the diagram are connected by double-headed arrows). Each of the stages will be discussed in more detail in the sections to follow.

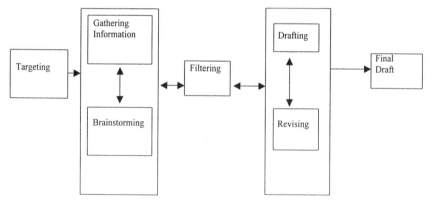

Figure 2-1 The Writing Process

Targeting

More writing has been ruined by failure to take into account its audience and purpose than by anything else. If you are writing, you are writing to *do* something, and you cannot accomplish that purpose without keeping it clearly in mind.

Gathering Information

Most writing tasks will require you to gather information of one kind or another; for some tasks, such as writing research papers, this will occupy much of your attention during the process. For any kind of writing, however, you *must* take into account your targeting decisions when gathering information. If, for example, you are asked to write an essay explaining to readers how to repair a lamp, digging up material on the history of electric lighting would waste your time (and your readers' if you included it). Instead, you would want to find material on current lamp designs.

As you begin your writing task, therefore, think about *what kinds* of information you need, and *how* you can go about getting them. Different sources of information are useful for different purposes, and you need to choose sources wisely.

Constantly review the decisions you make as you write. You may need to find new information to accomplish a purpose that did not occur to you at first, or you may decide that some of the material you originally intended to include is not as useful as you thought.

While you are gathering information, it is important to carefully document its **source**, so that you do not have to try to find it again later (see Appendix A).

Brainstorming

Brainstorming is the creative process of trying to generate as many ideas as possible without worrying whether your ideas are good or bad—you can make those decisions later. There are many different brainstorming techniques, ranging from making lists of ideas as they come to you to discussing things in groups to drawing diagrams with connected concepts. Different authors prefer different methods; use whatever works for you.

Filtering

At intervals, you will need to need to pause and look at the ideas you have generated while brainstorming and the information you have gathered, and decide what to discard.

Remember

Keep your audience and writing purpose in mind!

Organizing

Good writing is organized—it has a coherent structure that assists readers to make sense of what you are telling them. Part of the writing process, therefore, is deciding what order to present points in and how to let readers know when you are moving from one point to the next.

As with brainstorming, there are many different techniques for planning how to organize your writing. Formal outlines are one way to do this, but they are by no means the only way. If you find yourself worrying about whether to label something "5a" or "V(a)," you are not doing yourself any good. Worry about that later; while writing and revising, just use a consistent method that works for you. If the assignment requires a formal outline, you can always work on that later.

Drafting

This is the stage in which you sit down and actually write. There are three points you should keep in mind:

(1) **Just write something**. For many people, writing tasks (particularly large ones) are psychologically intimidating. If you go ahead and write something—anything—you will have gotten started, and every-

thing else will seem less dreadful.

(2) **Whatever you write does not have to be perfect the first time**. In fact, it can be awful; just make a note to come back to that part later. In particular, do not worry much about grammar and mechanics on early drafts—you can return to these points later.

(3) **You do not have to write sections in the same order they will be in the final version**. Introductions and conclusions can be the hardest parts to write; if you are having problems, just start with any section you feel most comfortable with.

Revising

This is the process of going back over your draft and improving it, thus producing a new draft. English courses frequently use terms like rough draft and final draft, but in reality there are as many drafts as you want. There are two strategies you will probably find useful when revising your draft:

(1) **Get comments from other people on the draft.**

(2) **Put it down for a day or two and then reread it**.

If you stare long enough at your own writing, you stop seeing it clearly, so you need outside opinions and an opportunity to get some distance from it. Of course, this also means that you should not try to write the whole thing the night before it is due.

Finalizing

Once the material is presented and structured the way you want, you can begin dealing with the details of grammar, mechanics, and format. Do you have any spelling mistakes? Do you need to have page numbers, and if so, where should they go?

This stage involves going over your draft again, but in a different way, looking at the language and presentation as well as the content to see if it all comes together to accomplish your original purpose.

Chapter 3
KINDS OF
WRITING

Writing Modes

Different kinds of writing serve different purposes, and picking the right mix of techniques will help you accomplish your goals.

Types of writing can be divided into *writing modes*. In each one you are trying to do something different:

(1) Description	Gives the reader a clear mental image of an object or event.
(2) Narration	Tells a story; gives the reader a clear understanding image of what happened in sequence over time.

11

(3) Comparison	Points out the similarities between two items or ideas.
(4) Contrast	Points out the differences between two items or ideas.
(5) Exposition	Explains complex or difficult concepts; helps readers understand a topic.
(6) Persuasion	Attempts to get the reader to agree with the writer about some topic.

You should view these writing modes as ingredients, not as ends in themselves. For any writing task, like composing a complaint letter or writing a research paper, you will need to use a mixture of the modes. Typically, you will use more than one mode—for example, you cannot do a good job of comparing two items unless you describe them first.

Below are checklists for each of the writing modes, as well as for some of the more common writing tasks you may be faced with in school and at work—comparison/contrast essays, essay exam answers, research papers, and opinion essays.

Checklists for Writing Modes

Description

- Use specific names and descriptive words and phrases (*jalopy, aquamarine, as large as a horse*) rather than general terms (*car, blue, big*) when possible.
- Use words and phrases describing spatial relationships (*in front, to the left*) so readers can easily understand where things are.
- If you are describing something complex, especially if it has multiple parts, imagine yourself moving around it or through it, using the movement to organize your description. For example, if you are describing a garden, think of yourself as walking through it.

What do you see first? What do you see next? Each stage of your walk can become a separate sentence or paragraph.

- Do not include predictable details. For example, you do not need to state that a car has wheels, since readers will assume that (although you may want to describe anything unusual about the wheels).

Narration

- Use words and phrases describing time relationships (*yesterday, then, next*) so readers will understand the sequence of events. However, avoid using the same time-words too often.
- Adopt a specific point of view and use it consistently. For example, if you decide to tell the story from your own viewpoint (using "I") and in present tense, stick with those choices.
- Most narration will include description as well, so also use the items on the description checklist above.

Comparison

- A comparison points out similarities that readers might not expect, or that might be important for a particular reason. Therefore, avoid writing about similarities that your readers will already know about (*both trains and cars are vehicles*) or that are not related to your writing purpose. For example, if you are comparing the styles of two painters, their use of different paints might be important, but the chemical formulas for the paints would probably be irrelevant.
- Starting with two items that most readers will consider completely *unlike* each other, and then proving that there are strong similarities, is a particularly good use of comparison.
- Comparisons usually involve descriptions and may incorporate narration as well.

Contrast

- The principles of contrast are similar to those of comparison, but you focus on differences instead of similarities. Do not point out differences that are completely obvious or that do not relate to your writing purpose.

- The best uses of contrast involve pointing out differences between items that most readers think are similar. Contrasting completely dissimilar items is, therefore, usually a waste of time.
- Contrasts usually involve description and may also incorporate narration.

Exposition

- Since exposition explains something to your audience that they do not already know, do not pick topics for exposition papers if you think your readers are familiar with them.
- If you have a great deal of specialized knowledge about a topic, you may find yourself assuming that readers know more than they actually do. This particularly becomes a problem if you use a lot of specialized terms. Ask yourself how many readers are likely to know the terms you use—or better yet, check with some friends and ask *them* if they already know those words. If they do not, be sure to include definitions.
- However, do not include definitions for terms your readers probably already know. It comes across as patronizing or as padding.
- Expositions draw on all of the previous writing modes.

Persuasion

- Since the point of persuasion is to influence the readers' opinions on an issue, do not pick topics that all of your readers agree on. For example, few readers need to be persuaded that smoking has at least some negative health effects. However, there is much disagreement about whether those negative health effects warrant government action.
- Readers have to believe that you respect them if you are to have any chance of persuading them to agree with you. Offer logical arguments against opposing positions, but avoid name-calling.
- It is particularly important to use a clear thesis statement in persuasion, since readers must know what your position is.
- Show that you have considered the opposing viewpoints carefully. Otherwise, readers may think that you do not agree with them only because you do not know enough.

- You want to end with a very strong piece of evidence or argument. If you have three or four pieces of evidence, use the strongest one last.
- Persuasion draws on all of the other writing modes.

Checklists for Writing Tasks

Comparison-Contrast Essays

- Typically, comparison is used along with contrast, since readers are often interested in both similarities and differences. When asked to compare and contrast, make sure you do both.
- Be sure to tell readers early in the essay what you think the most *important* similarities and differences are; use the rest of the essay to support those statements.
- There are two basic ways to organize a comparison-contrast essay. Both start with an introduction section (where you include the most important statements). After the introduction, you can choose either to (1) discuss everything about one item first, and then move on to the next item, or (2) pick one characteristic at a time, and then compare the two items on the basis of that characteristic.

   For example, if you were comparing and contrasting two cars, with the goal of explaining which one to purchase, you could have one section on each of the two cars, or you could choose to have a section comparing the cars' prices, then a section comparing the cars' safety records, and so forth.

Essay Examination Answers

- Focus directly on material that answers the question. This means you should avoid repeating the question and avoid including background material that does not directly relate to the answer. For example, imagine your test has a question like, "Many factors led to the Italian Renaissance. Which do you think are the three most important?" Here are some bad and good sample beginnings:

BAD (repeats question)

> "Many factors led to the Italian Renaissance. I think three were…"

BAD (unnecessary background)

> "The Italian Renaissance was the time of such famous figures as Leonardo da Vinci.…"

GOOD (direct answer)

> "The three most important factors were Italy's geographic position in Europe, its variety of political structures, and the lasting effects of the Black Plague."

- Make specific references, if possible, to material from both lectures and your readings.
- Include your main points in the first paragraph. If you run out of time to finish, the instructor will see that you knew the material but may just have been a bit slow in writing.
- If asked to agree or disagree with a position on some topic, keep in mind that you can frequently adopt a compromise position, partially agreeing and disagreeing with both sides.

Research Papers

- Organization is crucial in research papers. Make liberal use of organizing devices, including headings, section numbers, and the like.
- Most research papers are either expositions or persuasions. Make sure you know which kind the instructor wants. If you are asked to write a persuasion paper, do not write it as if it is an exposition.
- Do not let the research drive your paper—let your ideas and organization drive the research. A research paper should never be a collection of quotes and paraphrases held together by a loose framework of sentences. It should be an argument or explanation that *you* are making, with the researched material there to support *your* writing.

- Be careful not to include researched material that is off-topic or does not fit the section in which you use it. This looks like padding to instructors, who will suspect you included it just to make the paper longer.
- Time budgeting is vital to a good research paper. Many writers drastically underestimate the time needed to look through research material and decide what is relevant and what is not. At least half of the time spent on a research paper should be devoted to what you do *before* you start writing.

Opinion Essays and Letters to the Editor

- These are, of course, persuasive—or should be! Keep in mind that simply expressing your opinion on an issue is not usually sufficient to persuade people. You need reasons to back it up.
- Make your main point within the first ten lines, and use the rest of the essay or letter to back it up. Particularly when reading newspapers, readers skim articles, pausing only to read the entire piece if they are interested.
- Tone is particularly important in an opinion essay. Do not whine, and do not preach.

Chapter 4
COHESION AND COHERENCE

IN THIS CHAPTER:

✔ *Introduction*
✔ *The Paragraph Level*
✔ *The Essay Level*

Introduction

Writing is more than just the physical act of putting pencil to paper. It is the full process of creating something that communicates your knowledge and ideas to others.

Good writing needs to flow. The ideas you present should lead naturally from one to the next, and readers should not feel confused. In short, good writing needs to be *cohesive* and *coherent*.

Cohesion refers to how well your writing hangs together: Are all the sentences where they should be? Do sentences and paragraphs flow smoothly and sensibly from one to the next? Does the writing itself help your reader to understand your main points and supporting ideas easily?

Coherence, a closely related concept, refers to how well you provide clues for your readers so that they arrive at the destination you have in mind.

18

In English, we use certain devices at both the paragraph level and the essay (or research paper, or book) level to help readers along. These include:

- Using topic sentences and thesis statements to show readers the main point
- Using transitions to help readers know how to fit the parts together
- Using headings and paragraphs to let readers know where the boundaries between parts are

The Paragraph Level

Read the following example of a simple paragraph:

My dorm room last semester was a difficult place in which to study. First, the lighting was bad. There was no overhead light at all, and the lamp on my desk could only take a 40-watt bulb. There were no windows, so no sunlight came in. Second, my desk was too small for me to lay out my papers, and there were no drawers to hold things like pencils and paper. Finally, it was noisy. Even when my roommate wasn't barging in to tell me his stories, I could hear loud music coming from the rooms next door. After studying in a room like that, it's a wonder that I passed my classes!

Topic Sentence

In this paragraph the first sentence is the **topic sentence,** which tells what the paragraph will be about. We expect the rest of the paragraph to be about problems with the dorm room.

When you check your own writing, identify the topic sentence in each paragraph. After all, if you don't have a clear idea of what the topic is, it will be hard to ensure that every other sentence supports it!

Sometimes your instructor may ask you to find the topic sentence in paragraphs written by other people. While the topic sentence is often the first or second one, this is not always the case. For example, a topic sentence can come at the end of a paragraph, acting as a summary.

A good topic sentence expresses a clear and interesting opinion. It should help the writer decide what to include and help the reader predict what is coming.

> WEAK: I didn't like my dorm room last semester.
> STRONG: My dorm room last semester was a difficult place in which to study.

The strong sentence above gives more focus to the paragraph; the reader knows why the bad dorm room was a problem.

> WEAK: Tanisha is a very flexible person.
> STRONG: Tanisha's flexibility contributed even more to her success in college than her intelligence.

The strong sentence explains something about Tanisha's remarkable flexibility.

The rest of the sentences in the paragraph will support the topic sentence. They will explain, give examples, or add details. Check each paragraph carefully to see if the supporting sentences are about the subject in the topic sentence. If not, they should either be deleted or moved to another paragraph.

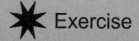 **Exercise**

Strengthen these weak topic sentences.

1. I'm glad I changed my major to history.
2. I had a bad part-time job last summer.
3. I'll never forget my last vacation.
4. This town's roads are (are not) good for bicyclists.
5. I (do not) prefer living with a roommate to living on my own.

Transitions

One device that helps your reader follow a train of thought is the use of transitions. These can indicate order (*first, second, next, then, after that, finally;* also *after that, before that, following this, meanwhile);* cause and effect (*as a result, because, since, so, therefore, thus*); and comparison or contrast (*likewise, similarly, although, however, in contrast, on the other hand, yet*). Be careful not to overuse transitions; you don't need one in every sentence. Use them to join complex ideas or to give structure to a long paragraph.

Pronouns

Read the following paragraph:

> Brittany and Ashley wanted to see a movie. They checked with the local theater, and there was one they wanted to see. After Brittany got some money at the bank, she picked up Ashley and they headed for the theater.

It would be annoying to repeat *Brittany and Ashley* every time we wanted to refer to the two girls:

> Brittany and Ashley wanted to see a movie. Brittany and Ashley checked with the local theater, and there was one Brittany and Ashley wanted to see.

It would be confusing, though, to use *she* or *her* in place of one of the girls if it wasn't absolutely clear which one was meant:

> After she got some money at the bank, she picked her up and they headed for the theater.

The Essay Level

Just as paragraphs in academic writing have topic sentences, the entire essay or research paper should have a **thesis statement**. Think of the thesis statement as telling the reader the point of your entire paper: Why are you writing it? What do you hope to show or prove? Then, just as each sentence in a paragraph adds supporting information to the topic sentence, each paragraph or section of your paper supports the thesis.

> **Remember**
>
> When checking your writing, skim to see if a name (like *Brittany*) or a noun (like *movie*) has been repeated several times; if so, see if a pronoun could be used instead. Then check your paper again, looking at the pronouns. Identify each noun they refer to, and see if there could be any confusion.

Remember that your thesis should be contained in one sentence. It should clearly indicate your opinion; a good test is to ask yourself if anyone could argue against your position.

WEAK: Colossal College had bad dorm rooms. The classrooms were small, too.

STRONG: In spite of the excellent academic programs at Colossal College, the poor facilities kept students from doing their best.

In the second example, the opinion is more focused (we know why *bad dorm rooms* and *small classrooms* were harmful), and the opinion is expressed in one sentence.

WEAK: Hunger is a problem in many parts of the world.

STRONG: World hunger could be avoided if citizens of developed countries followed a vegetarian diet.

The first sentence is not controversial; it is also quite general, and it doesn't indicate what exactly the paper will discuss. The second example gives a strong opinion and indicates what will be discussed in the paper: the reader knows that there will be a discussion of the diets of developed countries and how the results of changing that diet would affect world hunger.

In organizing your paper, make sure there are smooth transitions between paragraphs. This can be done by using a transition word or phrase (*therefore, meanwhile, at the same time*). Another way to do this is with parallel structure (for example, if you use a story to illustrate an advantage of something in one paragraph, you could also use a story to illustrate a disadvantage in the next paragraph). Pronouns are also used for transition. But be careful with pronouns — don't use a pronoun in the first sentence of one paragraph that refers back to a noun in the previous paragraph. Use the noun itself.

Chapter 5
FORMATTING

✔ *Formatting Styles*
✔ *General Guidelines for Formatting*
✔ *Visual Devices for Organizing Papers*

Formatting Styles

Formatting refers to the presentation of your final paper. The most common style types include:

MLA (Modern Language Association). Used primarily in the humanities, particularly in English classes.

APA (American Psychological Association). Used commonly in the social sciences, such as psychology and sociology.

"Chicago" Based on *The Chicago Manual of Style*, and used commonly in a number of disciplines for theses, dissertations, academic publications, and books. A shorter version of this style, usually called *Turabian* after its author, Kate L. Turabian, is frequently used for college classes.

These styles specify different ways to cite references, organize information in bibliographic entries, structure headings and subheadings for sections, and handle charts and tables.

Note!

Published guides are available for all of the styles mentioned above; you can usually find at least one copy in any public or school library. Do be sure, however, that you use the most recent version of the style guide. *The Chicago Manual of Style*, for example, is currently available in its fourteenth edition, and you should use that version rather than an earlier one.

General Guidelines for Formatting

Usually, instructors will either ask you to follow a specific style, like the ones above, or give you guidelines in class. If an instructor does not give you any guidelines, it is best to ask what style you should follow. That said, there are some rules that apply to all styles and that would be appropriate for just about any academic paper you will write in college.

- Type or word-process your paper. Some instructors will let you handwrite your first draft, but if at all possible you should type drafts from the beginning. For one thing, it will save you time on subsequent drafts. More importantly, you will find that it is much easier to rearrange paragraphs, cut sections, insert more text, etc., if you are working with a word processor.

- Double-space your paper. This makes it easier for your readers and also gives the instructor room to write comments. It is not true that if there is no space to write comments, the instructor won't write any and will think your paper is fine! Rather, he or she is going to feel annoyed.

- Leave at least a one-inch margin all around your text. This makes your paper easier to read and gives room for comments.

- Choose a normal font in a readable size. An academic paper is not the place for a bold, cute, or artsy font. Standard fonts for word processors include Times, Times New Roman, or Helvetica (also called Arial), in eleven or twelve point size. It's futile to try to change your font size or margins to pretend that your paper is longer or shorter than it really is. Always print your papers in black ink, on one side of the page.

- Don't justify your right margin. That is, don't set your word processor to line up all the right-hand ends of lines. While you will certainly see that done in books, with most word processors you will find that using a justified right margin results in uneven spacing between words in a line. Use instead the ragged right margin, where lines are of slightly different length.

- On the first page, write your name, the name of the class for which you are submitting the paper, and the date. Some instructors will ask you to use a separate title page; others will ask you to put this information in the upper right or left corner. It's advisable as well to put your name on each subsequent page, next to the page number, so that if the pages become separated your paper can be reassembled.

Visual Devices for Organizing Papers

Letting your readers know where they are and where they are going is one of the most important tasks you face as a writer. To accomplish this, you not only use *textual* cues (thesis sentences, transitions), but *visual* cues as well.

Distinct *headings* for sections and subsections are one of the most effective visual devices.

Although you don't need to use headings for short pieces of writing, they are extremely useful for research papers and longer essays. They let readers know when one section is finished and another begins, and if you use levels of headings, the readers will also know which sections go together. There are two things you should keep in mind about headings:

- Don't use a heading if you have only one subsection—that is what the title is for.

- Use consistent formatting in your heading levels. In other words, if you have decided that one major section should have a heading that is in italics and boldface, make sure all the other major section headings at the same level of organization are also in italics and boldface and are the same size type.

Some styles call for particular kinds of section numbering—legal style, for example, uses only numbers (1.1, 1.1.2, etc.). Other styles call for mixtures of numbers and letters (1A, 1B), or leave decisions about that sort of thing up to you. If you have been asked to use a particular style in your class, be sure to check whether it demands specific heading types.

Bulleted Lists are another common visual device for formatting papers. They are extensively used in business writing, but until recently were not found much in formal academic writing. If you are writing a research paper, it's a good idea to ask your instructor whether you can use bulleted lists or not. In any case, if you do use bullets in a class paper, don't use unusual ones—dots look okay, but small icons of dancing poodles just won't make the right impression.

Chapter 6
PARTS OF SPEECH

Introduction

Words can be divided into categories or *parts of speech*.

Some grammar books use different sets of categories, but for our purposes, we will discuss nine parts of speech:

- **Nouns**
- **Verbs**
- **Adjectives**
- **Adverbs**
- **Auxiliaries**
- **Prepositions**
- **Pronouns**
- **Conjunctions**
- **Interjections.**

Each of these categories represents a different kind of word—what grammarians call different *forms*. To a large extent, we assign words as parts of speech on the basis of what they do: nouns, for example, frequently refer to objects or concepts, and adjectives frequently provide more information about nouns.

It is important to recognize, however, that many words can do more than one kind of job. A noun that names a metal ("iron" for example) can also be used to tell the reader that another object is made from that metal ("an iron skillet"). Grammarians therefore make a distinction between *forms* (kinds of words) and *functions* (what the word does in a particular sentence).

We use the term *noun* for a kind of word, but the term *nominal* for anything that acts like a noun typically does. Likewise, *adjective* refers to a part of speech but *adjectival* refers to the kind of job that adjectives usually do. In "an iron skillet," we would say that *iron* is a noun that is behaving like an adjective—it is an adjectival noun.

Recognizing Parts of Speech

Nouns

Examples: Bob, desk, meatloaf

- Nouns *usually* refer to people, places, animals, objects, or ideas.

- Nouns are the only kinds of words that can be made plural or counted.

- Proper names (e.g. Bob, Lake Michigan) are always nouns.

- Nouns can also function as adjectivals (*an iron skillet*) or adverbials (*We leave tomorrow*) as well.

Types of Nouns:

Proper Nouns are given names for specific individuals or objects; they must be capitalized in writing.

Common Nouns are all nouns other than proper nouns.

There are two types of common nouns: *Count Nouns* can be counted (e.g. apples); *Mass Nouns* (also called *noncount nouns*) cannot be counted (e.g. sugar).

Verbs

Examples: eat, drive, become

- Verbs *usually* denote actions or conditions.

- If you think a word might be a verb, try forming a two-word sentence with it (e.g., *I ate*). If you can, the verb will be the second word. If you can't, try forming a three-word sentence ending in a noun (*I ate sandwiches*); if you can do that, the verb will again be the second word.

- You can also identify verbs by process of elimination. Only verbs and auxiliaries (helping verbs such as *will, should, is,* have) can be past tense, so if you can make a word past tense, and it's not an auxiliary, it's a verb.

- A verb can be used as a single-word answer to *What did she do?*

Types of Verbs

Verbs come in four basic types, sometimes called *principal parts*: *present, past, past participle, present participle*. These four types are important because they are the basis upon which all verb tenses are based:

  Present (examples: walk, drive)
   Can be used alone to express the present time.
   (*She eats lunch at the coffee shop.*)

   Used to make a statement that is true all of the time.
   (*Days are shorter in winter.*)

  Past (examples: walked, drove)
   Can be used alone to express past time.
   (*She ate lunch at the coffee shop yesterday.*)

Past Participle (examples: walked, driven)

For many verbs, the past participle looks exactly like the past tense. Some verbs, though (like "drive") have a past participle form that does not look the same as the past (compare "drove" and "driven").

The past participle can be combined with forms of "have" to make what are called *perfect tenses*: have walked, has driven, had eaten. The perfect tenses refer to actions that are thought of as being completed in some way. These actions might have been completed well in the past (*We had already eaten dinner*), be completed any time before the present (*We have already eaten*), or to be completed later (*We will have eaten*).

The past participle can be combined with forms of *be* make passive constructions—ones that focus on the person or thing affected by an action rather than the person or thing that performs an action (example: *Bob was given a raise*).

The past participle can also be used like an adjective, to provide more information about a noun (*The defeated candidate made a gracious concession speech*).

Present Participle (examples: walking, driving).

The present participle always has the "–ing" ending.

The present participle can be combined with forms of *be* to create what are called the *progressive tenses*—verbs that indicate that an action is thought of as continuing or ongoing. The action could have been continuing in the past (*We were eating dinner*), could be going on in the present (*We are eating dinner right now*) or could be yet to occur (*We will be eating dinner*).

Like the past participle, the present participle can be used like an adjective, to modify a noun (*The exhausting hike left everyone sore and sleepy*).

With most verbs, if you know one form, you can use simple rules to predict the others—these are called **regular verbs** (*drop, dropped, dropped, dropping*).

With other **irregular verbs,** which include some of our most common verbs, you have to learn the forms instead of being able to predict them (*write, wrote, written, writing* or *do, did, done, doing*).

Here are the principal parts for two common verbs, one regular (*walk*) and one irregular (*drive*):

Present	Past	Past Participle	Present Participle
Walk	walked	walked	walking (**regular**)
Drive	drove	driven	driving (**irregular**)

 **Note!**

When you look up a word in the dictionary, it is the **infinitive** you use to find it . The infinitive is simply a verb preceded by *to* (*to do, to go*) So, for example, you look up the word *be*, not *is* or *are*.

Adjectives

Examples: green, abundant, large

- Adjectives precede and modify nouns, typically by describing them or specifying how they are unique. Any given noun may be preceded and modified by multiple adjectives (*a **large old brown** shoe*).
- Adjectives answer the questions: *What kind is it?, How many?, or Which one?*

• Only adjectives can go in one of the following blanks: [*This is* _____ *-er than that is*], or [*This is more* _____ *than that is*]. For example: *This is greener than that is* or *This is more abundant than that is*.

Types of Adjectives

Comparative Adjectives
End in "–er" or are preceded by *more* and denote that one item has more of the quality than another item does. (*She is shorter than her brother.*)

Superlative Adjectives
End in "–est" or are preceded by *most* and denote that one item has more of the quality than any other. (*Jason is the tallest person on the team.*)

Adjectives can also be divided further into types based on meaning (color, size, etc.), since meaning affects what order they can occur in (people typically say *an old brown jacket*, but not *a brown old jacket*).

Adverbs

Examples: quickly, smoothly, always

• Adverbs answer the questions: *When? Where? Why? How often? In what manner?* or *To what extent?*

• Adverbs modify:
  Verbs (*She reads slowly.*)
  Adjectives (*They put on a really good show.*)
  Other Adverbs (*His talk went remarkably well.*)
  Sentences (*Read the recipe carefully.*)

• Many adverbs are made by adding an "–ly" suffix to an adjective. (*slow, slowly; beautiful, beautifully*)

- Adverbs can frequently be moved to the beginning or the end of the sentence without causing problems or a change in meaning.

Auxiliaries

Examples: will, should, is, have, might

- **Auxiliaries** or **helping verbs** are words that combine with main verbs to allow us to create complex verb tenses.

- The basic helping verbs are *be, have,* and *do.* English also makes use of a set of *modal auxiliaries* that allow us to express ideas like probability (*will, might, could*), obligation (*should, must*) and permission (*may*). Most of these modal auxiliaries can be used in more than one category, although there are limits. In spoken English, *may* can express probability (*It may rain tomorrow*) or permission (*You may leave early if needed*), but in highly formal situations it is restricted to the "permission" version.

- Questions that can only be answered with a *yes* or *no* always begin with an auxiliary.
  (*Does your home have a fireplace?*)

- Forms of *do* (do, does, did) are always auxiliaries.
  (*The manager does check his email daily.*)

- Forms of *be* and *have* are almost always auxiliaries if they are followed by another verb form or another auxiliary.
  (*I have heard of that new gallery downtown.*)

Prepositions

Examples: on, at, about, because of

- Prepositions are connecting words that express relationships of time, space, or purpose.

- Among the most frequent prepositions are *of, at, for, at, on, in, out* and *to.*

- A preposition can usually fill at least one of the blanks in the following sentences: [*Put this* _____ *that*], [*Move this* _____ *that*], [*We did this* _____ *that*].

- Prepositions are most often used to form prepositional phrases (see next chapter).
  (*Profits in the pharmaceutical industry have increased.*)

However, it is not uncommon for a preposition to combine with a verb.
(*She put up with the noise for only a week.*)

Types of Prepositions

While many prepositions are single words, clusters of two or even three words can fuse to form **phrasal prepositions**. The most common of these are *because of, out of,* and *in addition to.*

Pronouns

Examples: I, she, him, these, some

- Pronouns are used as substitutes for nouns.

- Pronouns are the only words in English that can have different forms depending on whether they are acting as subjects or objects. For example, you say *I saw him*, not *I saw he* or *Me saw him.*

Types of Pronouns

The most basic categories of pronouns are:

Personal pronouns (like *I, he,* or *them*), which stand for specific people or things

Indefinite pronouns (like *some* or *each*), which stand for people or things whose identity or quantity is not definite

Demonstrative pronouns (like *this* or *those*), which point at people or objects

Conjunctions

Examples: and, or, but, although

- Conjunctions are connectors between words, phrases, clauses, or sentences.

- A conjunction can usually go in one of the following blanks: [*Bob* ___ *Mary did that*], [*We saw a movie,* ____ *they wanted to stay home*], [____ *we leave, they will serve dinner*].

Interjections

Examples: Wow!, Ouch!, Oh, Darn it!

- Single words that you yell in moments of stress, surprise, or pain (when you hit your thumb with a hammer, for example) are almost always interjections.

- Words like *oh* and *well* that you say before actually producing a real sentence are interjections.

Rules of Usage

Rule One: Deciding Whether to Use an Adjective or Adverb. Although many English words can be used as more than one part of speech, many others cannot. Formal written English, in particular, demands that adverbs and adjectives be kept separate, although in speech, many people use *good* and *slow*—both adjectives—as adverbs. Here are some examples:

ERROR!	I did *good* on the test.
OK:	I did *well* on the test.

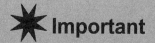 **Important**

If you cannot tell whether you need an adjective or an adverb, ask yourself what kind of question it would answer. Adverbs typically answer questions starting with *how did*, while adjectives answer questions starting with *how was* or *what kind of*.

How did you do on the test?
I did *well*.

How was your food?
It *was* good.

ERROR! You should drive *slow* here.
OK: You should drive *slowly* here.

Rule Two: Making Comparisons. If you want to form the comparative or superlative of a one-syllable word, you typically add a suffix (–er or –est) to the word (such as *old, older, oldest*).

Note: There are exceptions, such as the word *fun,* which, even though it is one syllable, should nevertheless be used with *more* or most. (*Going skiing was the most fun we had all year.*)

Two-syllable words are, unfortunately, unpredictable; most of them act like one-syllable words, but there are exceptions. (*Happy* can be either *happier* or *more happy.*)

Three-syllable words, on the other hand, are used with *more* or *most* in front of them (such as *more enjoyable* or *most enjoyable*).

Rule Three: Final Prepositions. Traditionally, ending a sentence with a preposition has been considered a major sin. In recent years, though, most modern style guides allow you to disregard this rule. However, you should be aware that some editors (and instructors) still follow it. It is simply something that you sometimes have to put up with.

Chapter 7
BASIC
PHRASE TYPES

IN THIS CHAPTER:

✔ *Introduction*
✔ *Kinds of Phrases*
✔ *Prepositional Phrases*
✔ *Verb Phrases and Verb Tense*
✔ *Rules of Usage*

Introduction

A *phrase* is a group of two or more words that lacks one or more of the elements that would make it a sentence such as a subject and verb.

It can be used like one of the parts of speech, such as a noun, an adjective, or an adverb.

This chapter gives you an overview of five basic kinds of phrases:
- **noun phrases**
- **adjective phrases**
- **adverb phrases**
- **prepositional phrases**

- **verb phrases**

This chapter also includes a discussion of verb tense, since tense is a characteristic of verb phrases.

Kinds of Phrases

Most phrases can be seen as a device for expanding a single word. For example, we could use several longer elements to stand for *Nick* in the following:

> Nick ate the apple pie.
> *That man* ate the apple pie.
> *That greedy man* ate the apple pie.
> *That greedy young man with the mustache* ate the apple pie.

All of these phrases are expansions of the word "man"—the phrases are essentially *man* and some other things to go with it. In this case, *man* is a noun, and so we call phrases built on it ***noun phrases***.

Noun phrases, like nouns, most often function as nouns in sentences. In other words, you can replace them with the words *something* or *someone*. However, noun phrases can have other functions as well. In the following sentence, the noun phrase is acting as an adverb, not as a noun.

> We eat lunch there *every Tuesday*.

Note that in this example, you cannot substitute *something* for *every Tuesday*.

Just as nouns can be expanded into noun phrases, adjectives can be expanded into ***adjective phrases***:

> I bought a *green* coat.
> I bought a *fluorescent green* coat.

and adverbs can be expanded into ***adverb phrases***:

He ran *quickly.*
He ran *very quickly.*

Not all phrases can be seen as simple expansions, however. There are two cases that merit special consideration: *prepositional phrases* and *verb phrases.*

Prepositional Phrases

Prepositional phrases are composed of a preposition followed by a noun phrase (or a gerund, which we will explain in a later chapter). The following are all prepositional phrases:

> *in* a moment   *with* some scissors
> *by* the lake   *because of* the weather

These all have the basic structure of a preposition plus a noun phrase (keeping in mind that *because of* is treated like a single preposition). Unlike the previous kinds of phrases, these do not seem to be expansions of a single word—it is rather difficult to see *in a moment* as simply an expansion of *in.* They do, nevertheless, form units that hang together but lack the potential to be sentences.

Prepositional phrases typically act like either adjectives or adverbs—in other words, they are adjectival or adverbial. Compare these two sentences:

> *On Tuesday,* we attended a concert.
> The concert *on Tuesday* was better than the first one.

In the first sentence, *On Tuesday* gives the reader more information about when the event happened—the phrase modifies the entire rest of the sentence and is therefore adverbial. In the second sentence, however, *on Tuesday* specifically modifies *the concert*—the phrase is there so you can distinguish that concert from another one. Here it is adjectival.

Verb Phrases and Verb Tense

Verb phrases are another special case. Some grammar books use the term *verb phrase* to refer to the main verb plus its auxiliaries. Others use the term to mean the same as *predicate*, which basically means everything in the sentence except for the subject (the next chapter will give you a more refined definition of both subject and predicate).

In this book, we will use the term *verb phrase* in its narrower sense—meaning the verb and any auxiliaries and adverbs that go with it.

You may have heard that English has three basic tenses (past, present, and future), or you may have encountered more complex labels, like *past perfect progressive*. It is important to note that tense is not always cut and dried. Consider the following pair of sentences:

> John *rides* his bike every morning.
> I *have finished* my paper already.

In the first sentence, *rides* is called *present*, even though you can say it when John is not even near his bike. In the second sentence, *have finished* is called a *present perfect*, even though the action it describes seems to be in the past.

To make sense of the labels, you need to understand **verb tense**, the property of the verb that expresses the time of the action, as in the past, present, and future.

It tells you the relation between the time of the action and the time you say the sentence.

English has just two special word forms for tense; present and past tense—for example, *walk* and *walked*. When we need to indicate future, we tack on an extra word or two (usually a modal auxiliary), like *will*, or *be going to*, or simply imply the future, as in *I leave for Lansing tomorrow*.

Another part of tense involves whether an action is thought of as finished or continuing through time. The "finished" view of an action is called the **perfect**, and involves using the past participle of a verb along with a form of *have* as an auxiliary—for example, *have finished, will have eaten*.

Present Perfect: I *have finished* my assignment.
Past Perfect: I *had finished* my assignment.

The "continuing" view is called the ***progressive,*** and it involves using the present participle of the verb plus a form of *be* as an auxiliary (*is going*).

Present Progressive: I *am driving* to Lansing.
Past Progressive: I *was driving* to Lansing.

Voice is another property of a verb, which refers to whether the verb phrase is ***active*** (the subject does the act) or ***passive*** (the subject is being acted upon) .
Here are some examples:

Active: Bob *saw* the suspect.
We *completed* the assignment.

In a passive verb phrase, the past participle form is used along with a form of the auxiliary *be*.

Passive: The suspect *was seen* by Bob.
The assignment *was completed.*

 **Note!**

- Although many passive sentences will contain a "by-phrase" (as with "by Bob" in the example above), the by-phrase is *not* a requirement. Many passives will not have a by-phrase at all.

- In spoken English, we frequently use a form of *get* instead of *be* to form passives (as in *My arm got broken*). Avoid this construction in formal writing.

The passive form is appropriate when you want to emphasize the *receiver* of the action. If you say *Bob hit John*, you are talking about what Bob did, but if you say *John was hit by Bob*, you are talking about what happened to John. Style guides frequently encourage writers to avoid the passive, because passives can be used to hide responsibility for a problem or produce stilted and awkward sentences. As with any grammatical construction, it is important to use the passive *appropriately*.

Mood

The property of a verb that indicates the attitude of the speaker toward what is being said is **mood**. The speaker could be expressing a fact, a wish, or a command. The words the speaker chooses indicates whether an action is real or unreal (something that is just imagined, or something that is just not true).

There are three moods:

Indicative
States a fact.
(*The contract has expired.*)

Imperative
Expresses a command or request.
(*Please let me know next week.*)

Subjunctive
Used after a main clause that expresses a demand, resolution, or wish.
I suggest he leave immediately.
We urge that this law be passed.

Used in *if, as if,* and *as though* clauses.
If I were president, I would outlaw that kind of thing.

While English does have some special forms for the subjunctive (like **were** in *If I* **were** *president*), we frequently just use modal auxiliaries to indicate that something is just a possibility or a wish (*it* **might** *rain tomorrow*).

Remember

This subjunctive form should only be used if the *if* part of the sentence is *contrary to fact.* In other words, use it when you are talking about what would happen if things were different—but they are not.)

Rules of Usage

Rule One: Using the Passive. Do not use *unnecessary* passives. Passives are very useful in a number of situations. If you are more interested in what happened to someone than who is responsible for it, or simply do not know who is responsible, passives are appropriate. However, you should avoid using passives just to hide responsibility.

Rule Two: Using Appropriate Verb Forms. When writing in Standard English, be sure to use the correct past tense and past participle forms when forming verb phrases.

ERROR:	She *drunk* her cup of coffee.
OK:	She *drank* her cup of coffee.

ERROR:	He *finished* his part before we arrived.
OK:	He *had finished* his part before we arrived.

IN THIS CHAPTER:

✔ *Introduction*
✔ *Subjects and Predicates*
✔ *Linking Verbs and Transitive vs.
    Intransitive Verbs*

Introduction

This chapter gives you an overview of subjects, predicates, and different kinds of objects. To avoid complicating matters too soon, only simple sentences are covered here. In later chapters, these concepts are applied to more complex sentence types.

Subjects and Predicates

How short can a sentence be in English? If you eliminate the kinds of things you say when you are answering someone else's question ("What did you eat for lunch?" "*Spaghetti*"), or giving people direct commands ("*Run!*"), you will find that the usual minimum size for an English sentence is two words:

> I slept.
> Gophers dig.

Each word in those little sentences fulfills a mandatory requirement in English sentences. When we speak or write, we typically say *something about something or someone*. The part of a sentence that names the person, place, or thing about which something is said is the **subject**. The part of a sentence that tells what the subject does or what is done to the subject is the **predicate**.

Subject	*Predicate*
I	slept.

Subject	*Predicate*
The man in the brown coat	sat down abruptly.

The subject is most often a noun or noun phrase. The predicate is, essentially, everything but the subject; it contains a verb form of some kind and can contain other parts of speech as well.

Finding Subjects

How can you identify the subject in a simple sentence? You may have been told that the subject is "the person or thing that performs the action in a sentence," but that is not always true. Consider the following (subjects are underlined):

> <u>Sean</u> suffered a heart attack.
> <u>Gina</u> was attacked by an angry dog.

It is highly doubtful that poor Sean set out to deliberately have a heart attack, and Gina is not portrayed in the second sentence as throwing herself at the dog. Sean *is*, however, whom the first sentence is about—the sentence is saying something about Sean, just as the second sentence is saying something about Gina. The reason subjects are frequently the person or thing performing the action in a sentence is that, as speakers, we are more likely to talk about who did something than what was done to them.

Even though the subject is not necessarily the first thing in the sentence, it is almost always the first *necessary* thing in statements (questions work a bit differently), and optional material that precedes it is sometimes set off by commas:

> In the morning, <u>we</u> left for Paris.

Notice that you can eliminate *In the morning* from that sentence entirely without changing the essence of the sentence.

Another characteristic of the subject is that it affects the verb in the predicate. Note the different endings on *eat* in the following:

> Ian *eats* dessert every evening.
> Mary and Jo *eat* pizza twice a week.

In Standard English, verbs in the present tense **agree** with the subject—they have a final –s or not depending on what the subject is.

Linking Verbs and Transitive vs. Intransitive Verbs

There are different kinds of predicates, and the differences have consequences. Consider the following two sets of sentences (the subject phrases have been underlined, and the verbs are in boldface):

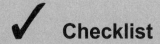

Checklist
Identifying Subjects

* The subject is typically the first necessary element in a statement.
* It is most frequently a noun or noun phrase.
* Present tense verbs agree with it.
* Optional material preceding it is frequently set off by a comma.
* It is not always the person or thing performing the action.

Set A   <u>Bruce</u> **sued** a real estate agent.
<u>My pet cat</u> **is sleeping**.
<u>Brenda</u> **asked** an executive a question.
<u>Someone</u> **has already tasted** my hamburger.

Set B   <u>My pet cat</u> **is** quite old.
<u>Brenda</u> **became** an executive.
<u>My hamburger</u> **tastes** strange.

The sentences in Set A all involve doing something (although the action involved can be rather low-energy or abstract). The sentences in Set B, on the other hand, all involve description or equivalence—they say that one thing is *the same as* another, or that one thing is *like* another—but they do not involve action in the usual sense.

Compare the two "hamburger" sentences, for example. *My hamburger tastes strange* does not describe what the hamburger is doing; it describes what the hamburger is, or is like.

Linking Verbs

The sentences in Set B all involve *linking verbs*, which are the various forms of *be, seem, appear, become* or some uses of verbs of the senses, such as *taste, smell, look , feel*. Linking verbs are followed by a word that renames or describes the subject. This element is usually called a *subject complement*:

Bruce is a real estate agent.
S   V   SC

He seemed quiet.
S   V   SC

Transitive and Intransitive Verbs

Two other types of verbs are:

Transitive
A verb that requires an object to complete its meaning.

The players *picked* the captain.

Intransitive
A verb that does not require an object to complete its meaning.

At the start of the play, our excitement *increased.*

Other examples:

The sign *fell* over.	**(intransitive)**
The wind *pushed* the sign over.	**(transitive)**

In the second sentence above, *the sign* is the **direct object** of the verb.

The wind pushed the sign over.
S   V   DO

There are two instances in which the differences among these types of clauses becomes important:

(1) In Standard Written English (especially in more formal writing), subject complements are treated differently than direct objects. Since subject complements are considered to rename or describe the subject, when a pronoun occurs as a subject complement, it takes the form it would normally take as subject (e.g. *I* instead of *me*). Few people follow this rule in *spoken* dialects of English, but it is considered proper in formal writing:

> The man in the white coat was he! (formal written)
> The man in the white coat was him! (informal spoken)

(2) English has a number of verb pairs in which one verb is intransitive and the other verb is transitive; in many cases, these sound similar and are frequent headaches for proofreaders. Below are a couple of examples. To determine which word to use, you must first decide whether the clause is transitive.

Intransitive:	The plate *sat* on the table.
Transitive:	He *set* the plate on the table.

Intransitive:	The plate *is lying* on the table.
Transitive:	He *is laying* the plates on the table.

Chapter 9
FULL CLAUSES
AND SENTENCES

Introduction

In the previous chapter, you learned that simple sentences are formed by combining subjects and predicates. Each of the examples you looked at contained one subject and one predicate. Yet, many English sentences are more complex than that.

We ate dinner early because we wanted to swim.

How would you deal with *because we wanted to swim* in that sentence? It seems to have a subject (*we*) and a predicate (*wanted to swim*), but there is already a different subject at the beginning of the sentence. Which subject counts?

51

The answer is that *both* subjects count, in their own way. We need some way of talking about sentences that have more than one subject + predicate combination. To do this, we need to introduce a part of a sentence that is intermediate between a sentence and a phrase: the *clause*.

Clauses come in two basic types: *full clauses,* which consist of a subject plus a full predicate, and *reduced clauses* (sometimes called verbal phrases or nonfinite clauses), which are formed with a reduced predicate, and which lack a full subject. In this chapter, we will discuss full clauses and how they are combined into sentences. Reduced clauses will be discussed in the next chapter.

Kinds of Full Clauses

Since some of the grammar rules used in formal writing are sensitive to differences among several types of clauses, it is important to be familiar with them.

Independent and Dependent Clauses

The most important distinction is between *independent clauses* and *dependent clauses*. Fortunately, the difference is fairly straightforward: an **independent** clause can be used by itself as a sentence and sound finished, while a **dependent** clause has to rely on another full clause accompanying it. Compare the following:

Set A: my guest ate a sandwich
            the deer bounded into the forest
            the picture was hanging on the wall

Set B: because the weather was lousy
            which we could not find
            that the fuse had been lit

Which set sounds more like sentences? In Set A, all that is really necessary to get sentences is to capitalize the first letter, stick a period on the end, and you are done. The clauses in Set B, on the other hand, sound unfinished—they might work if there were other material with them, but they cannot be sentences by themselves. The clauses in Set A are independent, while those in Set B are dependent.

Dependent clauses are further subdivided according to the function they serve. The three basic types are ***noun clauses***, ***adjective clauses***, and ***adverb clauses***.

Noun Clauses

Noun clauses can substitute for noun phrases and frequently act as the subjects or objects of verbs:

> Harry said *a word*.
> Harry said *the tide had come in*.

Noun clauses are very common with verbs like *think* and *say* and *feel*, since they allow the speaker to present an entire idea or statement as an object—you normally *say* whole sentences, not single words.

There are two basic types of noun clauses. The first kind starts with the word *that* (although you can omit the *that* in many cases), and are common with verbs such as *say*.

> He says *that the performance was a success*.

The second type starts with a word like *what* or *whatever* and are common with verbs such as *ask*.

> He asked *what time the movie started*.

Adjective Clauses

Other dependent clauses can give you more information about particular nouns in other clauses; these are called ***adjective clauses*** or ***relative*** *clauses* (there is no difference between the two; some grammar books use one label while others use the other). There are many situations in which using a simple noun might confuse people. Imagine, for example, that you hear the following in a crowded room:

> Please talk to the person.

Since there would be a number of people to choose from, this would be a bit vague. Instead, you are more likely to hear something like the following:

> Please talk to the person *who is wearing the uniform.*

The adjective clause *who is wearing the uniform* modifies *person* in this case. People frequently use adjective clauses when the hearer will be confused without one. Sometimes, however, adjective clauses are used as a quick way to toss in more information, even if the hearer would not be confused without it:

> Mr. Halloway, *who operated the machine for thirty years,* knew its every quirk.

If there is not more than one Mr. Halloway, the adjective clause in this case gives extra information, not required information.

Adjectival clauses that give *required* information are called **restrictive**,

> The newspaper *that was delivered yesterday* was incomplete.

while ones that give *extra* information are called **nonrestrictive.**

> Her latest article, *which deals with alternative medicine,* has received a lot of attention.

There is a punctuation rule that hinges on the difference between restrictive and nonrestrictive clauses, so it is important.

Adjective clauses typically begin with a word like *who, whom, which,* or *that,* although this element is optional in some cases:

Did you know the man *whom* Mr. Holt fired?
Did you know the man Mr. Holt fired?

This element, when present, is called a ***relative pronoun***, and there are several rules presented later in this chapter that deal with choice of relative pronoun.

Adverb Clauses

The third major type of dependent clause is the ***adverb clause***, so called because it provides more information about a verb in another clause, or (more frequently) provides more information about another clause as a whole. Clauses that tell you the conditions (when, why, or where) under which another event occurred are frequently adverb clauses:

> We canceled the picnic *because it rained.*
> I looked up *when I heard the loud noise.*
> *Although his foot hurt,* Carl kept walking.

 **Note!**

Adverb clauses are also called ***subordinate clauses*** in many grammar books. Other grammar sources frequently use "subordinate clause" as an equivalent to "dependent clause."

Adverb clauses begin with words such as *because* and *although*, which are known as ***subordinating conjunctions***. Some words, like *because* and *if*, are always subordinating conjunctions (and so make good clues if you are looking for adverb clauses), but others, like *before*, have other functions as well:

> Before I ate dinner, I washed my hands.
> Before dinner, I washed my hands.

Before I ate dinner is an adverb clause—it has a subject (*I*) and a full verb (*ate*). *Before dinner*, on the other hand, is just a prepositional phrase.

You Need to Know

How to distinguish dependent clause types:

- You can frequently substitute the word *something* or *someone* for a noun clause and the sentence still sounds possible (He said *that the movie started early* / He said *something*).
- Adverb clauses can be moved—you can rearrange the sentence so that the adverb clause is at the beginning or the end without changing the basic meaning of the sentence (Before we ate lunch, we went swimming / We went swimming before we ate lunch). You cannot do this with adjective or noun clauses.
- A dependent clause starting with *what* or any of the " –*ever*" words (*whatever, whoever,* etc.) in Standard Written English will be a noun clause.

Sentences

Sentences are usually classified in two different ways: based on their internal complexity (simple vs. complex, vs. compound, vs. compound-complex), and based on the function that the grammatical structure of the sentence is most suited for (statements vs. questions vs. commands).

Simple, Complex, Compound, and Compound-Complex Sentences

One way to describe sentences is based on combinations of independent clauses and dependent clauses. The most basic kinds of sentences are composed of one independent clause; these are called *simple sentences*:

> [We canceled the picnic].
> IC

It is possible to have a long sentence that, nevertheless, contains just one clause:

> [In front of the fireplace, my parents put a large carved wood chest with brass hinges decorated with designs of ivy and maple leaves].
> IC

Since you can add any number of prepositional phrases to a simple sentence, it can become lengthy.

You can also combine two independent clauses by putting a conjunction like *and* or *but* between them; the result is called a *compound sentence*:

> [I ate a sandwich], and [Karen had a salad].
> IC1   IC2

Another combination is an independent clause and one or more dependent clauses—a *complex sentence*:

> [I ate a sandwich] [because it looked delicious].
> IC   DC

Finally, if you combine two independent clauses and one or more dependent clauses, you get a *compound-complex sentence*:

> [[I ate a sandwich] [because it looked delicious]],
> IC   DC
> and [[Karen had a salad] [because she was on a diet]].
> IC   DC

For most writing purposes, of course, you can get by quite happily without knowing whether a sentence is compound or complex. There are some punctuation rules that involve the types, however.

In addition, most good writers use a *variety* of sentence types, so labels like *compound* and *complex* can be useful for analyzing your own writing. If something you have written looks boring for some reason, it may be because you are using the same kind of sentence over and over again.

Remember

Labeling the sentence types in your writing can draw your attention to how much variety (or lack of it!) you are using.

Statements, Questions, and Commands

Another way of classifying sentences is based on what they are primarily used for. Most of the time, when we produce a sentence we are stating something, asking a question, or giving a command of some sort. Thus, we have three basic kinds of sentences:

- *statements* (also called *declaratives*)
- *commands* (also called *imperatives*)
- *questions* (also called *interrogatives*)

These categories correspond to some differences in the sentences' structure. Commands, for example, are the only kind of sentence in English that let you leave out the subject. We can say things like *Take out the garbage* or *Run!* because the hearer always knows the subject is *you*.

Questions involve rearranging the sentence and sometimes adding words like *who* or *why*. They are further subdivided into **yes/no questions** (called that because their answers are either *yes* or *no*) and **wh-questions** (which usually start with a word beginning with "wh-"). Here are some examples:

Statement: He ate a sandwich.

Y/N Question: Did he eat a sandwich?
WH-Question: What did he eat?

Command: Eat that sandwich!

It is important to realize that the terms refer to grammatical structure, not to the *ultimate* purpose of the sentence. We frequently use questions, for example, to give polite commands (*Could you pass the salt?*), and we can use a statement as a question if we use the right intonation.

Rules of Usage

Rule One: Do Not Use Fragments in Formal Writing. Do not use a dependent clause or a simple phrase by itself as if it were an independent clause. If you do, the dependent clause or phrase is called a *fragment* and will usually be considered a mistake.

> ERROR: We ate early. Because we wanted to swim.
> OK: We ate early because we wanted to swim.

Rule Two: Do Not Create Run-On or Comma-Splice Sentences. Do not combine two independent clauses unless you use either a conjunction (such as *and, but, or*) or a semicolon between them. If this mistake is made, the result is a **run-on sentence**, or, if you use a comma, a *comma splice.*

> ERROR: I saw a movie Mary stayed home. (Run-on)
> ERROR: I saw a movie, Mary stayed home. (Comma Splice)
> OK: I saw a movie, but Mary stayed home.
> OK: I saw a movie; Mary stayed home.

Rule Three: Only Use *in Which* Where it is Appropriate. Do not use *in which* as if it is merely a more formal version of *which* or *that*—it should only be used if the relative pronoun actually follows the prepo-

---

⭐ **Note!**

- Fragments are most common with adverbial clauses, particularly those starting with *although* or *because*.
- If you have problems with fragments, try reading each sentence of your paper *out of order.* Fragments only sound good when they immediately follow the sentence they should be part of—when you disrupt the order, you can more easily notice they are fragments.
- The fragment rule applies primarily to formal writing. In more informal or creative writing, *deliberate* fragments are allowed for emphasis.

---

sition *in* in the relative clause. Even where *in which* is appropriate, be careful not to repeat the *in.*

Rule Four: Use the Correct Relative Pronoun. Several rules govern the choice of relative pronouns. Below are the commonly accepted uses—and misuses—for frequent relative pronouns.

that   Used in **restrictive** relative clauses when the word it stands for **does not represent a human.** *The coat that I left at the restaurant was very expensive.* You can frequently omit *that* entirely: *The coat I left at the restaurant was very expensive.*

which   Used in **nonrestrictive** relative clauses when the word it stands for **does not represent a human.** *The Supreme Court building, which was designed in neoclassical style, is very imposing.*

who   Used in both restrictive and nonrestrictive relative clauses when the word it stands for **represents a human** and **acts as the subject or subject complement in the relative clause.** *The man who spoke to me was Mr. Smith.*

whom   Used in both restrictive and nonrestrictive relative clauses when the word it stands for **represents a human** and acts as **an object in the relative clause**. *The person whom I spoke to was Mr. Smith* (or more formally, *The person to whom I spoke was Mr. Smith*). In informal writing, people usually use *who* for *whom*, but it is advisable to err on the side of caution until you are sure the people who will be reading your work allow this.

whose   Used for any possessive, whether human or not. *The woman whose purse we found was grateful we returned it.* Just be sure you do not confuse *whose* with *who's*, a contraction for "who is."

Chapter 10
INFINITIVES, GERUNDS, PARTICIPIAL PHRASES, AND ABSOLUTE PHRASES

IN THIS CHAPTER:

✔ *Introduction*
✔ *Infinitives*
✔ *Gerunds and Participials*
✔ *Absolute Phrases*
✔ *Rules of Usage*

Introduction

In this chapter we will discuss four kinds of reduced clauses:

- *infinitives*
- *gerunds*
- *participial phrases*
- *absolute phrases*

These kinds of clauses lack a subject and do not have complete predicates. In other words, they do not have a subject in the normal sense, and although each of these types of clauses has a verb form, it is not a full verb and would need an auxiliary to be complete.

Each of these different types of incomplete clauses have different uses, and formal grammar has a few rules that treat them differently. Below, we will describe the types, their uses, and the rules that involve them.

 **Note!**

There is some disagreement about what to call these constructions. Some consider any group of words lacking a subject and a complete predicate to be a phrase—so you will see terms like *infinitive phrase* or *gerund phrase*. Others call them *reduced clauses*.

Infinitives

An infinitive is the simplest form of the verb—the form you use to look up the word in the dictionary. Instead of looking up *was* or *were*, for example, you look up *be*. For most verbs, the infinitive is the same as the present tense, but without any possibility of having the "–s" ending that you could otherwise get with third person singular subjects.

Most infinitives occur with the word *to* in front of them as well, which in this case is not usually considered a preposition. An infinitive can be just *to* plus a verb form, or it can be *to* plus an entire predicate:

> to eat
> to eat spaghetti for dinner

Infinitives can be nouns—serving as subjects or objects in a sentence—adjectives, or adverbs. Here are some examples of different uses:

Noun Subject:	*To walk on river ice* is not a good idea.
Noun Direct Object:	I wanted *to watch a movie.*
Adjective:	The machine was a device *to open cans.*
Adverb:	I opened the door *to get some air.*

Infinitives can take on any function of a noun except as the object of prepositions.

By far the most common use of the infinitive is as the direct object of particular verbs, like *wanted* in the example above. In fact, these infinitives are so closely tied to their verbs that you may be tempted to think the verb is *wanted to watch.* Most, however, consider the infinitive as a direct object.

The use of the infinitive as an adverb can frequently be paraphrased as *in order to.*

Infinitives can occur with a noun in a *for*-phrase that is interpreted roughly like a subject:

> It is difficult *for **him** to move all those rocks.*

Even though *him* in that sentence is interpreted as performing the action of moving the rocks, it is not really considered a subject. Notice, for example, that you cannot use *he* (the subject pronoun); you are required to use *him* (the object pronoun).

Gerunds and Participials

Modern English grammar has inherited some uses of terminology from traditional grammar. One of these involves the distinction between gerunds and participial phrases. The same construction can be a gerund in one case and a participial phrase in another. Latin had different forms for the two, and early English grammarians thought that we should pretend that English did, too.

Here is how the system works:

- A *gerund* (sometimes called a *gerund phrase*) is a verb form ending with the "–ing" **used as a noun**. It can occur as subject, direct object, indirect object, subject complement, object complement, or object of a preposition (e.g. *before leaving for work*).

- A *participial* is either the present or the past participle of the verb **used as an adjective or adverb** (e.g., *the jacket hanging on the door*).

In other words, if you have a reduced clause with an "–ing" verb form in it (for example, *sitting in that chair*), you cannot tell if it is a gerund or a participial phrase without first deciding what the reduced clause is doing in the sentence.

If it is acting as a subject or object, it is a **gerund**.

Sitting in that chair makes my back hurt.

If it is acting as a modifier, it is a **participial phrase**.

The guy sitting in that chair is my brother.

Like infinitives, gerunds can appear with a word or phrase that the reader or listener interprets roughly as the subject:

***John's** taking the test* surprised everyone.

Even though *John* is interpreted as performing the action of taking the test, it is not really a grammatical subject. If you substitute a pronoun for *John* here, you cannot use *he*; instead, you must use *his*:

> **His** *taking the test* surprised everyone.

Absolute Phrases

Absolute phrases are phrases that function as an adverb. They consist of either a noun phrase followed by a participial, or a noun phrase followed by another noun phrase or prepositional phrase:

> *Her work having been finished*, Ellen left for home.
> *Her father a free man at last*, Ellen was able to claim victory.

In general, an absolute phrase expresses some condition or situation that is useful for interpreting the sentence it accompanies. Absolute phrases are typically placed at the beginning of sentences, although they may occur at the end as well.

Rules of Usage

Rule One: Do Not Split Infinitives. Traditionally, writers were told not to split infinitives—in other words, not to put any words between the *to* and the verb form. For example, *to boldly go* is a split infinitive. More recently, many grammarians have recommended relaxing this rule, especially in cases where *not* splitting the infinitive would be confusing or awkward. Check with your instructor, though, before assuming that you can split an infinitive without getting into trouble.

Rule Two: Use Possessives with Gerunds in Formal Writing. The subject-like element that sometimes occurs with gerunds has traditionally been required to be possessive (*I was surprised by John's/his taking the test*), even though English speakers typically use a nonpossessive form in speech (*I was surprised by John/him taking the test*). This is another rule that is in contention; many grammarians recommend ignoring it if following it sounds awkward. Ask your instructor for his or her policy, to be on the safe side.

Rule Three: Avoid Dangling Modifiers. Since participial phrases lack subjects, readers will typically interpret the nearest noun phrase as being their understood subject—sometimes with humorous results:

> OOPS! Having received a black belt in karate, the excited puppy was easily subdued by George.

It sounds as if the puppy has studied karate, rather than George. This kind of problem can usually be solved by rearranging the sentence:

> OK: Having received a black belt in karate, George easily subdued the excited puppy.

This kind of problem can also occur with other kinds of modifiers, particularly prepositional phrases that have gerunds as objects of the preposition:

> OOPS! After burning to the ground, the insurance inspector examined the house's ashes.

> OK: The insurance inspector examined the house's ashes after it burned to the ground.

Chapter 11
CONJUNCTION

IN THIS CHAPTER:

✔ *Introduction*
✔ *Basic Conjunctions*
✔ *Types of Conjunctions*
✔ *Linkage*
✔ *Comparison and Ellipsis*
✔ *Rules of Usage*

Introduction

A *conjunction* is a word or phrase that serves as a connector between words, phrases, clauses, or sentences.

People seldom think in little chunks—our thoughts usually connect with each other, and we realize that there are relationships between ideas. Language enables us to reflect these connections; in fact, when we do not indicate such connections, our language seems awkward or choppy. Compare the following two paragraphs:

- We had scheduled a picnic for Monday. We did not have the picnic. It rained on Monday. We rescheduled it for Tuesday. Some of us could come on Tuesday. Some of us could not come on Tuesday. We had two picnics. One was on Tuesday. The other was on Wednesday.

- Although we had scheduled a picnic for Monday, we did not have it because it rained that day. We tried to reschedule it for Tuesday, but some of us could come that day, and others could not. Eventually, we had two picnics—one on Tuesday and one on Wednesday.

The second paragraph sounds much more like real language, because the structure of the sentences and the words chosen in some cases clearly indicate the relations among the ideas.

Part of this chapter will discuss the types of conjunctions. Distinguishing between the types is important because, although informal spoken English and Standard Written English draw on much the same grammar, there are some important differences between the two in the ways in which constituents can be connected together.

Basic Conjunctions

All three of the following sentences describe the same situation, but they differ in certain ways:

1. Leslie and I saw a horror film, but our friends went to an action movie.
2. Leslie and I saw a horror film although our friends went to an action movie.
3. Leslie and I saw a horror film. However, our friends went to an action movie.

In the first sentence, there are two independent clauses—*Leslie and I saw a horror film* and *our friends went to an action movie* — joined by the word *but*. In terms of grammar, the independent clauses are the same. They are both **independent clauses**; neither clause outranks the other.

This is an example of *coordination*, and the word that joins the two clauses (*but* in this case) is called a *coordinating conjunction*. The basic pattern for coordination is as follows (keeping in mind that IC stands for "independent clause"):

[IC], coordinating conjunction [IC]

In sentence number two, an independent clause is joined with a dependent clause—*Leslie and I saw a horror film* can stand on its own as a sentence, but *although our friends went to an action movie* cannot. The independent clause can be thought of as outranking the dependent clause. This is an example of *subordination*, and the word that converts the second clause into a dependent clause (*although* in this case) is known as a *subordinating conjunction*. The basic pattern for subordination is as follows (DC stands for "dependent clause):

[IC] [DC (subordinating conjunction + clause)]

The subordinated clause is an adverb clause of the type discussed in the previous chapter. Grammarians do not consider uses of nominal or adjectival clauses to be examples of conjunction.

The example in sentence number 3 actually involves two sentences. Both of them are independent clauses, but they have not been combined into a single sentence. Instead, a word in the second sentence (*however* in this case) tells the reader what the relation between the sentences is. This is an example of *linkage*.

Words representing relationships in linked sentences (like *however* in this example) go by different names in different grammar books; the two most common terms are *adverbial conjunction* or *connective*. We will use *connective* in this book. Although the connective can actually occur in different places, it is most commonly at the beginning of the second sentence, giving us the following as a basic pattern:

[Sentence]. [Connective, Sentence].

Types of Conjunction

Coordination

Coordination involves any case in which the two or more words being joined are of the same type. They do not have to be independent clauses. In fact, the most common cases of coordination involve simple nouns or noun phrases:

> We bought pears and other fruit at the market.

Both *pears* and *other fruit* are nouns or noun phrases, and both of them are doing the same thing in the sentence—serving as direct objects of *bought*. Any words or group of words can be combined this way, as long as they are of the same type.

Predicates:
> They [[bought some popcorn] and [saw a movie]].

Verbs:
> He [[peeled] and [ate]] some shrimp.

Adjectives:
> It was a [[dark] and [stormy]] night.

Dependent clauses:
> Larry skipped dinner [[because he was busy] and [because he wasn't very hungry]].

Of course, you are not limited to joining two items at a time; we use coordinating conjunctions to construct entire lists:

> We bought bread, milk, sugar, eggs, and vegetables.

There are seven coordinating conjunctions in English:

- **for**
- **and**
- **nor**
- **but**
- **or**
- **yet**
- **so**

Of these, only four are always conjunctions—*and, or, nor*, and *but*. The other three all have other functions as well: *for* is usually a preposition, not a conjunction; *yet* is most often an adverb; and *so* can act more like a subordinating conjunction (particularly when it can be replaced with *so that*). Here are some examples to help you distinguish the uses:

Coordinator:	He left in a hurry, **for** the weather was turning nasty.
Preposition:	He bought a book **for** his grandmother.

Coordinator:	The car looked new, **yet** it was not very expensive.
Adverb:	Is it time to eat **yet**?

Coordinator:	The linebacker had been injured, **so** the coach brought in a new player.
Subordinator:	We propped open the door **so** (that) the wind could come in.

There is an additional category of coordinating conjunction called the **correlative conjunction**. These are two-word conjunctions such as "either...or," "neither...nor," and "both...and." For purposes of analysis, both parts of the correlative conjunction are considered to be the same conjunction—just split in two.

Subordination

There are many more subordinating conjunctions than coordinating conjunctions, perhaps because the main purpose of subordinating conjunctions is to enable the writer to be more specific about the relations between clauses.

A good part of learning to use subordination effectively is learning the precise usage of each subordinating conjunction; you cannot just throw in *because* where you really need an *although*.

An important point to remember about subordination is that the material in the subordinate clause—as with material in dependent clauses in general—is being presented as background material. It is perceived as less important than the material in the main clause and is presented as if it is not open to question. Thus, you should avoid putting your main points in subordinate clauses.

Linkage

Linkage is particularly useful when you are dealing with groups of related ideas. You can assemble the ideas into chunks with coordination and subordination, and then use linkers to relate the chunks to each other. This prevents readers from having to try to hold something like a twenty-clause sentence in their heads at the same time. Examine the following:

Although many people assume that buying a house is always preferable to renting one, buying is not a good idea in areas in which property values are dropping. Therefore, it is always a good idea to check property rate changes when looking for a house, since you cannot make a good decision without such information.

There are a number of related ideas in the above sentences. They all could have been handled by subordinating conjunctions, but the result would have been a very long sentence, and readers might have trouble putting the ideas together in the right way.

Most readers appreciate a break in the middle of complex arguments like that, and using a connective like *therefore* has an additional advantage: it shows the reader how the ideas group together:

[[Although 1], [2]]. [Therefore, [[3], since [4]].

Think of making a pie. There are a number of ingredients, but you cannot just throw them all in a bowl and stir—you would get a gooey mess. You first need to combine some ingredients to make the crust, and other ingredients to make the filling. Only after you have made the crust and filling separately can you assemble them into a pie. Used together, coordination, subordination, and linkage can provide an "assembly plan" for the reader, much as a pie recipe provides an assembly plan for a cook.

Scientific writing tends to make heavy use of linkage. Connectives such as *however* and *on the other hand* are far more common in technical writing than in speech (which tends to use more coordinators). Part of learning to write professional-sounding technical prose is mastering the use of connectives.

Comparison and Ellipsis

There are many occasions in speech and writing when you need to compare one item with another in terms of a quality—"X is larger than Y," for example, or "X is more expensive than Y." These are called *comparative constructions* and are considered to involve a kind of conjunction, with *than* being a subordinating conjunction.

An important point about comparative constructions is that we usually leave material out of them. Compare the following:

We ate more food than Bob.
We ate more food than Bob ate food.

Everyone understands that the two sentences mean the same thing, but the second one is awkward, because it repeats information needlessly. The term *ellipsis* is used for cases such as this in which material is understood but left out.

Understanding ellipsis in comparatives is important because it lets you avoid some situations that might be confused if you use the wrong pronoun. Compare these awkward sentences:

> Glen gave Lisa more candy than I gave Lisa candy.
> Glen gave Lisa more candy than Glen gave me candy.

The proper elliptical versions of these would be as follows:

> Glen gave Lisa more candy than I did.
> Glen gave Lisa more candy than me.

In spoken English, people tend to use object pronouns (me, him, her) instead of subject pronouns (I, he, she) after *than*, regardless of what is actually meant. This can be confusing in some cases—if you hear, "Glen gave Lisa more candy than me" in spoken English, you might not know which of the two interpretations to pick. In formal writing, being careful with subject versus object pronouns prevents such confusion.

Rules of Usage

Rule One: Coordinated Structures Should Be Parallel. The elements joined by coordinating conjunctions must be of the same type; that is to say parallel. Mismatching forms produces what is called a *parallel structure fault*. You cannot join an adjective and a noun, or an independent clause and a dependent one.

> Error: We walked slow and carefully.
> OK: We walked slowly and carefully.

> Error: We left early, for the movie was boring and because we had to get up early.

> Better: We left early because the movie was boring and
>   because we had to get up early.
> Best: We left early because the movie was boring and we
>   had to get up early.

Pay particular attention to this rule if you are using correlative conjunctions, since they are the source of most mistakes with coordination:

> Error: We talked both [to the landlord] and [the tenant].
> OK: We talked to both [the landlord] and [the tenant].

In the first sentence, there is a prepositional phrase in one part and a simple noun phrase in the other. The corrected version has parallel noun phrases, both serving as the object of the preposition *to*.

Rule Two: Do Not Repeat Elements Unless Necessary. Do not repeat elements unless you need to—if you can collapse a conjunction, do so:

> Poor: Jennifer ate some plums, and she ate some cheese.
> Better: Jennifer ate some plums and cheese.

For some purposes, however, you might want to have long, drawn-out coordinated elements, especially if you are trying to give an impression of exhaustion ("I had to read six books, and I had to write two papers, and I had to do an experiment, and..."). As with most grammar rules, the key here is that you need a good reason to break it.

Rule Three: Use the Proper Subject and Object Forms in Comparisons. In formal writing, always distinguish subject pronouns from object pronouns in comparisons, picking the correct one for the meaning you intend (see the section on comparisons and ellipsis above). You can easily do this by trying to add a "did" at the end—if it works, then you should be using a subject pronoun:

> OK: Jan ate more ice cream than I.
> OK: Jan ate more cream than I did.
>
> ERROR: Jan ate more ice cream than me.

Chapter 12
AGREEMENT AND CONSISTENCY

IN THIS CHAPTER:

✔ *Introduction*
✔ *Subject-Verb Agreement*
✔ *Consistent Use of Pronouns*
✔ *Consistent Use of Verb Tenses*
✔ *Consistent Use of Major Sentence Types*
✔ *Rules of Usage*

Introduction

Formal written English places a high value on consistency: once you choose a particular pattern or strategy, you should change it only if there is a good reason to do so. The following pair of examples have usages that are common in spoken English but are considered problems in written English:

77

If you see someone trying to use that sidewalk, warn them that the cement is not set yet.

So, I'm talking to this guy, and I tell him that we're going to leave early. And he said he didn't want to.

Both sentences have consistency problems (and the second sentence also has an informal use of *so*). In the first sentence, the pronoun *someone* is picked up in the second clause with *them*—but *someone* is singular, and *them* is plural.

In the second sentence, the speaker switches from present tense (*I'm talking, I tell*) to past tense (*he said*) without any clear reason for doing so. If you are telling a story, once you pick present tense or past tense, you should stick with that tense and only change when there is a reason.

Matching verbs and subjects in number—singular or plural—is another example of this principle of consistency. If you use a singular subject, you should use a singular verb; if you use a plural subject, use a plural verb. Sometimes violations of **subject-verb agreement**, as this is called, are obvious—we might notice them even in spoken English:

I are very upset with my grammar grade.

Other cases are more subtle, however:

Each of the students were pleased with their grammar grades.

In the example above, *each* is considered to make its noun phrase singular, so *were* should be *was* (and *their* should be *his/her*). Since the word next to the verb is plural in that example (*...students was/were...*), it is easy to make a mistake.

Note!

In many cases, the rules governing written English seem different than the ones governing spoken English, so they have to be learned consciously.

Subject-Verb Agreement

Subjects and verbs must match in number. To make things even easier, whether a verb is singular or plural is not even always relevant. Unless the main verb is in present tense, is a form of *be*, or has *be* or *have* as an auxiliary, the singular and plural are identical.

> I *go* to the store every Tuesday.
> He *goes* to the store every Tuesday.

but

> I *went* to the store every Tuesday.
> He *went* to the store every Tuesday.

There are, unfortunately, factors that spoil this otherwise rosy picture. The most common complications are caused by one of the following:

- Very long and complex noun phrases as subjects
- Indefinite pronouns in subject noun phrases
- Coordinated subjects
- Nested clauses or phrases

The problem with long, complex ***noun phrases*** is the burden they put on your attention span: by the time you get to the end of the noun phrase, you may have lost track of whether the main part of it was singular or plural. Consider the following:

> **The box with the wooden frame like the ones we saw in the corners of the rooms in the lower level of the temple complex during the archeological dig** is probably a ceremonial object.

The entire boldfaced portion of that sentence is a noun phrase—although one with an embedded relative clause and lots of prepositional phrases—and is acting as the subject of the sentence. By the time a reader gets to the main verb *is*, the fact that the head of the noun phrase is *box* has probably been forgotten.

If you find yourself getting bogged down in a long subject phrase, the best approach is to look at the predicate instead. Turn it into a question focusing on the subject, and allow yourself only a short answer. For example, you could turn the sentence above into the following:

> *What* is probably a ceremonial object?

The short answer would be, "the box." This technique simply lets you focus on the important part of the subject—the part that determines if it is singular or plural.

Indefinite pronouns cause a different kind of problem. Some begin subject phrases that are always plural:

> *Many* of the students *were* excited about the new uniforms.

Others are variable—whether or not the phrase is singular or plural depends on the noun following the indefinite pronoun:

> *Some* of this pie *is* still cold.
> *Some* of these pies *are* still cold.

Still others begin phrases that are always considered singular, even if the noun that follows is plural.

> *Each* of the pies *was* still cold.

It is this last "always singular" category that most often causes problems. It would not be surprising if you thought that *each of the pies were still cold* sounds acceptable—it is a common construction in spoken English. In written English, however, it is considered a mistake. A good technique for dealing with this is simply to scan your writing for uses of *each* and *one*, and then make sure your agreement is correct.

Coordinated subjects are the third major source of agreement errors. Obviously, when you join two nouns, whether singular or plural, with *and* you get a plural:

> John *is eating* dinner.
> John and Mary *are eating* dinner.

You probably will not make mistakes with *and*, unless some other factor (like an indefinite pronoun) is involved. The conjunction *or* is a bit more complicated, though. The rule for formal written English is that the verb agrees with whichever of the coordinated elements is closer— even if the result sounds awful:

> Either the coach or the team members are making a mistake.
> Either the team members or the coach is making a mistake.

Most people would want to use *are* in the second sentence, because it would sound more natural, but that would be a mistake in formal writing. The best approach to this problem is to put the plural item second, so you can use the better-sounding plural verb legally.

There is a related problem with expressions like *as well as* or *in addition to* that are frequently used like *and* but that are set off by commas. Words introduced with these conjunctions do not count as far as subject-verb agreement is concerned:

> The coach, as well as the team members, was making a mistake.

Again, using this rule may produce sentences that are formally correct but awkward-sounding. Keep in mind that it is not illegal to simply reword the entire sentence so as to avoid the problem entirely.

Consistent Use of Pronouns

Whenever you write even one sentence, you probably find yourself using pronouns (in fact, *this* sentence has four in it). Often, you use several different kinds in the same sentence—using *she* or *her* to refer to a woman and *he* or *him* to refer to a man, for example:

> Mary wasn't sure what Bob was up to, but *she* was determined to catch *him* at it.

This kind of pronoun shifting is perfectly acceptable; in fact, if you did *not* shift pronouns, you would be making a mistake.

However, there are also situations in which you might start using one kind of pronoun and then lose track of it, shifting to a different kind without a good reason. In spoken English, we frequently shift to using *they* or *them* when it is technically incorrect:

> *Every student in the room* nervously looked at *their* tests.

Every student is singular in that sentence, so connecting *their* to it is a needless shift. The sentence would be better rewritten so that the subject noun phrase is plural:

> *All the students in the room* nervously looked at *their* tests.

The extremely formal use of *one* to mean "any person" frequently causes this kind of problem:

> *One* should always be careful to keep *your* knives sharpened, since *you* could otherwise injure *yourself.*

Once you start using *one* in this way, unfortunately, you are locked into it. You must continue using it in some form:

> *One* should always be careful to keep *one's* knives sharpened, since *one* could otherwise injure *oneself.*

For most purposes, you are better off simply avoiding this ultra-formal use of *one*.

Consistent Use of Verb Tenses

Just as there are good reasons to shift from one kind of pronoun to another when writing, there may be good reasons to shift from one verb tense to another—but there are also times when you might find yourself shifting when you should not. For many writing tasks, you have to decide whether to use present tense or past tense. When telling a story, for example, you can decide to tell it as if it is happening now, or tell it as if you are remembering a past event. The key is to stick to that choice—if you shift from present to past for no reason, you will confuse your readers. Once you have chosen a tense, you can use different tense patterns to organize the events you are describing:

> *Past Tense Narratives*: Use simple past tense for the main events, past perfect tense for background events that happened before the story began, and past progressive tense for ongoing activities that are interrupted by the main events. Use *would* or *might* to introduce events that might happen later.
> *Example:* I *got up* this morning and *discovered* that my front right tire *had gone* flat. While I *was changing* it, I *realized* that I *would be* late for work.

> *Present Tense Narratives*: Use simple present tense for the main events, present perfect tense for background events that happened before the story began, and present progressive tense for ongoing activities that are interrupted by the main event. Use *will* or *may* to introduce events that might happen later.
> *Example:* I *get up* this morning and *discover* that my front tire *has gone* flat. While I *am changing* it, I *realize* that I *will be* late for work.

One of the most frequent situations that causes problems with tense consistency is shifting from direct to indirect quotations. Direct quotations can have any tense in them, but indirect quotations have to match tenses with the main part of the sentence. Usually, this involves shifting tenses into the past (again, words like *will* and *may* change to *would* and *might*):

> He said, "I *think* I *will get* some apple cider."
> He said he *thought* he *would get* some apple cider.

In formal writing, when you shift something that is already past tense further into the past, use past perfect:

> He said, "I *finished* the painting."
> He said he *had finished* the painting.

Consistent Use of Major Sentence Types

Although different kinds of conjunctions allow you to combine clauses into compound or complex sentences, you should avoid shifting from one major type (statement, question, or command) to another in mid-sentence. The following example is a bit awkward:

> My steak is overcooked, and could you get me another one?

It starts off as a statement, and then changes abruptly. Making it two separate sentences would solve the problem.

The most frequent source of type shift problems is indirect questions in quotations. Although *directly* quoted questions have the grammatical structure of a regular question, *indirectly* quoted ones do not, and often have the grammatical structure of a statement:

> OK: He asked, "Where did I leave the car keys?"
> ERROR: He asked where did he leave the car keys?
> ERROR: He asked where he left the car keys?
> OK: He asked where he left the car keys.

Note that the problem can involve punctuation as well as grammar—the third sentence has the right structure, but should not have a question mark at the end. It sounds as if the speaker is not sure whether he *asked* about the car keys or not.

Rules of Usage

Rule One: Verbs Must Agree with their Subjects. If the subject is singular and the verb is present tense, it must end with an –s suffix or be the appropriate form of an irregular verb (*is, has*). The verb *be* must appear as *am* in present tense if the subject is *I*.

Rule Two: Pronouns Should Agree with their Antecedents. The *antecedent* is the word that a pronoun substitutes for; pronouns must match this antecedent. Do not use a plural pronoun, like *they*, to stand for a singular phrase, like *the student*.

Rule Three: Use Tenses Consistently. Do not change verb tenses without reason. If you start in present tense, stay in present tense unless there is a good reason to change.

Rule Four: Use Sentence Types Consistently. Do not change from a statement to a question, or vice versa, in the middle of a sentence. *Direct quotations* are an exception to this rule, but *indirect quotations* are not.

 **Note!**

Some spoken dialects of English use different forms of the verbs *be* and *have* in the present tense. For Standard Written English, the correct forms are as follows:

	Singular		Plural
I	*am / have*	We	*are / have*
You	*are / have*	You	*are / have*
She/He/It	*is / has*	They	*are / have*

Chapter 13
VARYING SENTENCES

IN THIS CHAPTER:

✔ *Introduction*
✔ *Common Sentence Variants*

Introduction

In the previous chapters, you learned about subjects and predicates and about different ways to combine clauses to form sentences. However, English affords enormous flexibility in sentences, and not all of it can be explained by saying that we can combine different kinds of clauses. Consider the following sentences:

> I gave Matt some advice yesterday morning.
> Yesterday morning, I gave Matt some advice.
> Matt was given some advice yesterday morning.
> It was Matt whom I gave some advice yesterday morning.
> What I gave Matt yesterday morning was some advice.
> What did I give Matt?
> Give Matt some advice!

These could *all* be considered variations on a theme. Good writers do not use variations randomly, however, and each one of those sentences would be more appropriate in some contexts than in others. This chapter describes some of the more common ways of varying sentence patterns and gives you pointers on when they are particularly useful. However, one of the best ways to learn the art of crafting sentences is to pay careful attention to what other good writers do and try your hand at it yourself.

Common Sentence Variants

Adverb Elements: Introducers, Interrupters, and Enders

Adverb elements in a sentence can usually be moved to different places in the sentence without drastically affecting the sentence's meaning. In general, there are three major "landing spots" for such adverbials, labeled A, B, and C below:

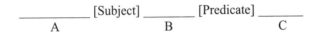

For our purposes, we are giving them the following names: Items that go in blank A are *introducers*, those in blank B are *interrupters*, and those in blank C are *enders*. The following three sentences illustrate the word *however* in all three positions:

> However, Octavian managed to become emperor.
> Octavian, however, managed to become emperor.
> Octavian managed to become emperor, however.

The subject of those sentences is *Octavian*, and the predicate is *managed to become emperor*. The adverb connective *however* can act as an introducer, an interrupter, or an ender.

Introducers give readers information that allows interpretation of the rest of the sentence—they are organizing devices. For example, if you are writing a description of a house, you will probably need to tell readers where objects are, and so you will need to use phrases like *in the living room* or *in the kitchen*. These adverb prepositional phrases would make excellent introducers, since they would then provide a framework for the reader ("*In the living room,* we saw several chairs."). Words, phrases, and entire adverb clauses can all act as introducers.

If you use an interrupter, you are focusing attention on the subject of the sentence; the interrupter characterizes the subject in some way:

> We wanted pizza. However, Bob wanted Chinese food.
> We wanted pizza. Bob, however, wanted Chinese food.

The second sentence focuses more attention on Bob—you can almost see the writer looking annoyed that Bob, alone among everyone else, was demanding a different kind of food. Interrupters tend to be fairly short as a rule, although they may even consist of phrases:

> Bob, just to be annoying, wanted Chinese food.

Enders have a quality of afterthought about them. You have already completed your statement and are adding something to put a slight spin on its interpretation.

> We wanted pizza. Bob wanted Chinese food, however.

Using *however* as an ender in the sentence above does not really single Bob out as an exception. Instead of implying that Bob is being difficult, it simply conveys the idea that the vote was not unanimous.

Passives

Passive sentences give you a way to make the subject of a sentence the person or object affected by the action in a sentence. This is particularly useful if you are more concerned with what happened *to* someone or something, than what someone or something *did*:

A car hit George!

George was hit by a car!

Most people are more interested in what happens to the victim in an accident than in the object that caused the accident, so a passive sounds perfectly acceptable in this case. Passives are also useful if you do not *know* who or what caused an action and that information is not very relevant:

Kangaroos are found in Australia.

We do not really care who finds the kangaroos in this case. The passive sentence is much more natural than an active counterpart:

Anyone looking for kangaroos finds them in Australia.

If you are writing about kangaroos, you will usually want to make kangaroos the subject of your sentences—and that means you may need to use passive constructions. Keep in mind that a passive sentence does not need a "by somebody" phrase—it is the verb that makes the sentence passive.

As mentioned earlier, you should avoid using passives unnecessarily, particularly if they obscure responsibility.

Chapter 14
WORD CHOICE

Introduction

Which of the following would you be more likely to say?

> "I'd like a steak with grilled onions."
> "I'd like a slab of cooked cow with onions."

There is no real grammatical difference between the two sentences—they both involve the structure "I would like [noun phrase]." Instead, the difference lies in the words that were chosen. Even though a steak may be correctly defined as a slab of cooked cow, logic does not really matter in this case. One sounds good, while the other does not.

Issues of word choice in writing fall under the heading of *diction*. There are some general rules for diction that work in all situations, but you should know up front that if you approach diction as a set of rules to memorize, you will fall short. Because words in English can be used in so many different ways, there are as many rules than there are words. How, then, do writers become proficient at choosing the right words? The answer is quite simple. Writers learn diction from long exposure to other people's writing. In short, you learn how to choose words by *reading*. Writers who have a mature command of diction are invariably those who have consistently read a wide variety of material—newspapers, novels, essays, and so forth.

General Rules for Diction

Rule One: Avoid Redundancy. Redundancy involves using the same word repeatedly when there are other options available. While you must frequently use words like *the*, you should avoid repeating content words (like *bench*) if you can gracefully avoid them. One of the primary functions of pronouns is to allow you to refer back to something without repeating it, so use pronouns if the reader will not be confused by them. Another good tactic is to use synonyms—*bench* and *seat* are quite interchangeable for many purposes.

Rule Two: Be Aware of Common Word Problems. Some words, such as *affect* and *effect*, are easily confused. There is a list of such words in the appendix; look it over, and if you know that you have problems with particular words, make a point of checking your writing.

Rule Three: Be Specific. If you use general words like *stuff, aspect,* or *facet* in your writing, readers might not know exactly what you mean. Worse still, they may get the impression you are not really saying anything at all. Whenever possible, be specific. For example, instead of saying *I have some issues with several aspects of this assignment*, say *I'm not sure I understand the directions, and I don't have access to some of the readings*.

Rule Four: Do Not Include Definitions for Terms You Know Your Readers Will Understand. Defining common terms like *automobile* usually is not necessary unless you are introducing a different kind of definition than your readers are expecting. Simply defining something they already know about makes you look like you are padding your writing.

Rule Five: Include Defining Material if You Think Your Readers Will Not Know Particular Words. In some situations, especially when writing academic papers, you may find that you need to use *jargon*— vocabulary that is specific to a particular job or field of study and which most people do not use. If your writing is likely to be read by some people who do not know these words, include short statements or definitions so that they can understand your jargon.

Rule Six: Avoid Inflated Phrases. Bureaucratic language is known for using many words in any situation where one will do. Unfortunately, inflated phrases like *at this point in time* (instead of *now*) and *achieve closure* (instead of *finish*) have crept out of bureaucracy and into public language. If you do not have a good reason for using a long phrase, use a shorter one. In particular, avoid *doublespeak*—inflated phrasing that deliberately misleads people. An employee who has *undergone a motivated job-transfer experience* has simply been fired; it is unfair to both the employee and the general public to call it anything else.

Rule Seven: Avoid Nonwords. Nonwords are invented words that are used in place of already existing ones which usually work better. Good examples are *to orientate* (the verb *to orient* works just fine) and *analyzation* (the noun form *analysis* is far superior).

Rule Eight: Be Aware of the Emotional Tone of Your Words. While English has plenty of words that are completely neutral (like *bench*), it also has words that are inherently positive (*reasonable, progress*) or negative (*senseless, barbarous*). When you use one of these charged words, make sure you are using it *for a reason*. Your word choice can make a letter sound angry—and that can be a problem if you did not *mean* for it to sound angry. This is especially true in writing e-mail messages.

Chapter 15
PUNCTUATION

Introduction

Perhaps you've seen the joke that was being sent around by e-mail a few years back. A teacher gives her class the following sentence to punctuate:

woman without her man is nothing

The boys capitalize the first word and stick a period at the end, to get

Woman without her man is nothing.

But the girls add a few more marks, and come up with

Woman! Without her, man is nothing.

The point is not that the battle of the sexes is still being fought (at least in e-mail), but rather that punctuation is a powerful tool. You need to use it correctly to give your sentences meaning, and the meaning that you intend! Even if you feel confident about using punctuation, you should take the time to review the rules in this chapter, and promise yourself to review your own writing carefully at least once just to check punctuation. It's easy to make careless errors, and computer spell checkers can't help with misplaced apostrophes.

Rules

Period

A period comes at the end of a statement:

> I'm going to Idaho this summer.
> I want a sandwich.

If the sentence ends with an abbreviation, don't use more than one period:

> RIGHT: My cousin is finally getting his Ph.D.
> WRONG: My cousin is finally getting his Ph.D..

Question Mark

A question mark comes at the end of a question:

> What's the capital of Idaho?
> Have you seen my sandwich?

Use a period, not a question mark, if the question is embedded in a statement:

> I don't know what the capital of Idaho is.
> I have no idea who took my sandwich.

Use a question mark if the sentence is grammatically a question, even if the purpose is something else (in the following example, the sentence is really a suggestion or an offer):

> Why don't you sit down?

Exclamation Point

An exclamation point comes at the end of a sentence that shows a strong emotion like surprise or excitement.

> Would you look at all those birds!
> I didn't take your sandwich!

 **Note!**

Exclamation points are more common in casual writing, such as letter to friends. Use them sparingly in academic writing. You may, of course, use them in writing dialogues:

> INFORMAL: The capital of Idaho is Boise!
> FORMAL: "Please don't ask me what the capital of Idaho is!" cried the child.

Never use more than one exclamation point:

> WRONG: Hey, that's my sandwich!!

Comma

Remember that the purpose of commas is to make your sentence clear and easy to read. They do this by marking *boundaries* of different types. Consider:

> WRONG: While I was batting Tony was catching.
> RIGHT: While I was batting, Tony was catching.

If you read the first sentence without realizing that there is a kind of boundary after *batting*, you might think that it was poor Tony who was getting batted.

While some of these boundaries are at points where you might pause to take a breath, it is not true that you should put a comma everywhere you would pause for breath. For example, no matter how long or hard it is to pronounce a subject, you should never put a comma between it and a predicate if there is no interrupter:

> WRONG: The letter on the table by the door, was for me.
> RIGHT: The letter on the table by the door was for me.

Commas are frequently used to mark boundaries in series. Use a comma to separate a series of three or more items:

> I can't eat butter, ice cream, or cheese.

> Collecting stamps, reading books, and making models are my brother's hobbies.

Use a comma to separate three or more adjectives of the same type:

> There's a strange, smelly, furry animal under our porch. (These are all the same type of adjective: they describe a quality of the animal.)

However, don't use a comma to separate adjectives of different types:

> It has four sharp black claws on each foot. (These are different types of adjective: number, quality, and color.)

Can you fit the word *and* in between the adjectives (strange *and* smelly *and* furry animal)? Can you change the order of the adjectives (smelly, strange, furry)? Then use commas. If you can't (four *and* sharp *and* black; black sharp four claws), then don't.

Use a comma before a coordinating conjunction to separate two independent clauses. Coordinating conjunctions are *and, but, or, nor, so, for,* and *yet.*

> I was already running late, so I skipped breakfast.
> He didn't study at all, but he still got an 87 on the test.

> ## Remember
>
> Don't put commas before the first item in a series, or after the last one:
>
> WRONG: I can't eat, butter, ice cream, or cheese.
>
> WRONG: I can't eat butter, ice cream, or cheese, with out getting sick.
>
> RIGHT: I can't eat butter, ice cream, or cheese without getting sick.

Don't use a comma after a coordinating conjunction:

WRONG: I was already running late, so, I skipped breakfast.

Remember: Coordinating conjunctions don't always separate independent clauses. Don't just sprinkle commas in your sentences whenever you see them.

WRONG: I'm not afraid of bugs, or mice.
RIGHT: I'm not afraid of bugs or mice.

WRONG: Katie stopped by the bank to cash a check, and then drove to the dry cleaner's to pick up her dress.

RIGHT: Katie stopped by the bank to cash a check and then drove to the dry cleaner's to pick up her dress.

Use a comma after any *introducer* that is more than one or two words long:

By the way, your mother called.

This rule particularly applies to *adverbial clauses* used as introducers, since they are more complex:

Unless it rains, please put the cat outside.

By the time I arrived, most of the guests had already gone home.

Use a comma before and after a nonrestrictive word, phrase, or clause:

My roommate, Susan, is very untidy. (I have only one roommate, and her name is Susan.)

Don't use commas before and after restrictive segments:

My roommate Susan is very untidy. (I have more than one roommate, but only Susan is untidy.)

In General: Use commas after *introducers* over one or two words long, use commas before and after *interrupters*, and use a comma before an *ender*. Use commas to separate items in a series, and to set off nonrestrictive modifiers.

Test to see if a clause is restrictive or nonrestrictive by taking it out. Does the meaning of the sentence change? If the meaning doesn't change, the segment is nonrestrictive: use commas. If the meaning does change, the segment is restrictive: don't use commas.

Semicolon

Using semicolons correctly can make your writing seem more academic or formal.

Use a semicolon to connect independent clauses that are closely related:

> I'm not going to invite James to my party; he didn't invite me to his.

Using a comma in the above sentence would create a *comma splice*; this means that there isn't enough of a break between the two sentences. It is possible to put a period after *party* and start a new sentence, but the semicolon shows that the second independent clause has a strong connection to the first.

Semicolons are commonly found in sentences that use transitional words and expressions such as *after all, as a result, for example, however, in addition, in fact, therefore,* and *thus.* The sentence used above as an example could be more elegantly expressed as

> I'm not going to invite James to my party; after all, he didn't invite me to his.

Don't use a comma after a coordinating conjunction:

> WRONG: He finished waxing the car; but, completely forgot about changing the oil.
>
> RIGHT: He finished waxing the car, but completely forgot about changing the oil.

Use a semicolon to separate a series of three or more items if *those* items already contain commas:

> This semester I'm taking biology, which meets in the morning; chemistry, which meets in the afternoon; and a seminar in psychology, which meets once a week in the evening.

Colon

Use a colon to introduce a list:

> There are three kinds of movies I would watch anytime: quirky comedies, old black and white dramas, and mysteries.
>
> We need to order the following supplies: paper clips, legal pads, staples, and clipboards.

Don't use a colon immediately after a verb:

> WRONG: The three chores I hate most are: washing the dishes, cleaning the bathroom, and taking out the trash.
>
> RIGHT: These are the chores I hate the most: washing the dishes, cleaning the bathroom, and taking out the trash.

Use a colon to introduce an explanation:

> It's pretty easy to take care of these fish: just feed them once a day and change the water when it gets dirty.

Use a colon to introduce a quotation from a source, but not quoted dialogue:

> RIGHT: I'll never forget the advice my mother always gave me: "It is better to be rich and healthy than poor and sick."
>
> WRONG: Carla said: "Please take your clothes out of the dryer, so I can put mine in."

Apostrophe

An apostrophe can indicate that a letter or number has been taken out:

> don't = do not (the second "o" is missing)
> Class of '04 = Class of 2004 (the "20" is missing)

However, contractions (*can't, don't, I'm, shouldn't,* etc.) are not usually used in academic writing; they are too informal. They may be used if you are writing dialogue, or quoting someone directly.

Some style guides suggest using an apostrophe to make the plural of individual letters and numbers:

> For some reason, I write sloppy G's.
> Small children sometimes mix up their 6's and 9's.

However, some style guides do *not* use an apostrophe to make these kinds of plurals. It is best to check the style guide for your discipline, or ask your instructor which method to use.

An apostrophe can indicate possession:

> Jane's opinion = the opinion of Jane
> workers' compensation = the compensation belongs to the workers

Proper names that end with an *s* usually take an apostrophe and an additional –s when possessive:

> Mr. Hess's order = the order of Mr. Hess

The two most frequent exceptions to this are *Jesus'* and *Moses'*.

An apostrophe frequently means a letter has been taken out; put the letter back in, and see if the sentence makes sense.

> The cat was cleaning it's fur.

> Does it make sense to say *The cat was cleaning it is fur*? No. So use *its*.

In addition, be careful with these often-confused pairs:

> **you're** (= you are) vs. **your** (possessive pronoun)
> **they're** (= they are) vs. **their** (possessive pronoun), and even **there** (indicating a place)

One common mistake is to use an apostrophe to form the plural of a noun.

WRONG: She has lot's of kittens to find homes for.

 **Note!**

Be careful using apostrophes with singular and plural nouns. With singular nouns, the apostrophe comes before the *s*. With plural nouns, the apostrophe comes after the *s*, (if the plural is formed with an *s*, of course).

The student's papers = one student
The students' papers = two or more students
The children's room = two or more children

- Be careful using two possessives in one sentence; make sure you know how many things belong to how many people!

Jason and Jennifer's car = the car belongs to both Jason and Jennifer
Jason's and Jennifer's cars = Jason has a car, and Jennifer has a car

- The possessive pronouns **whose, yours, his, hers, its, ours,** and **theirs** don't use apostrophes. Be careful with contractions that sound like these possessive pronouns:

it's = it is vs. **its** (possessive pronoun)
who's = who is vs. **whose** (possessive pronoun)

Test each apostrophe in your writing. Using the sentence above, for example:

—Does *lot's* represent a missing word (*lot is? lot was?*)?
—Does *lot's* indicate possession (does *kittens* belong to *lot?*)?

If neither of these makes sense, which is the case here, you shouldn't use an apostrophe.

Quotation Marks

Use quotation marks to show the exact words someone spoke:

> The professor said, "If you don't turn the paper in by Friday, I won't accept it."

Don't use quotation marks if you are paraphrasing what another person said:

> The professor said that if I don't turn in the paper by Friday, she won't accept it.

That, as used in the sentence above, for example, usually indicates that the remark is not a direct quote.

You Need to Know

If you are using a quote that will be more than five lines in your paper, indent the entire quoted section five spaces from each side, and do not use quotation marks around it. It should also be single-spaced, even if the rest of your paper is double-spaced.

If you are using expressions like *he said* or *the girl remarked* after the quote, then use a comma and not a period at the end of the quoted sentence:

> "We're going to study the history of Texas," announced the teacher.

Use a period if the quoted sentence comes at the end:

> The teacher announced, "We're going to study the history of Texas."

Notice how a comma is used after *announced* in the sentence above to introduce the quote.

Periods and commas are placed inside quotation marks. Semicolons go outside the quotation marks. Exclamation points and question marks may come inside or outside, depending on whether they are part of the quote or part of the surrounding sentence:

> "Does anyone know where the Alamo is?" asked the teacher.
> Do you know who said "Remember the Alamo"?

Sometimes you may quote someone who is quoting someone else. Then, use single quotation marks around the quoted quote:

> The teacher asked, "Do you know who said 'Remember the Alamo'? "

Capitalize the first letter of the word that begins a quote. But if an expression like *she said* interrupts the quote and divides the sentence, then don't capitalize the first word of the part that finishes the quote:

> "Today," said the teacher, "we are going to study the history of Texas."

Notice the comma after *today,* which separates the quoted material from the other part of the sentence.

Use a capital letter only if the second part is a new, complete sentence:

> "We'll start studying the history of Texas today," explained the teacher. "It will take us at least a month to cover the early part."

Parentheses

Parentheses can be used to enclose information that is not part of your main idea, like an aside:

> I'm not going to the party, because I don't have time (and besides, I don't have a thing to wear).

However, this is less common in formal, academic writing than in informal writing such as letters or e-mail.

You will, however, use parentheses when citing sources:

> I don't know what I'd do without my *Schaum's Easy Outline of Writing and Grammar* (Spruiell and Zemach, 2001).

Dash

Like parentheses, dashes enclose material that adds to the main sentence, but are somewhat more formal than parentheses. Use them sparingly, and they can be effective.

> Now that I've mastered the use of quotation marks—as well as the other forms of punctuation—I feel more confident about writing term papers.

If you are using a typewriter, make a dash with two hyphens: --
If you are using a word processor, use the em-dash, which is a longer line: —

Ellipsis

An ellipsis can indicate an unfinished sentence:

I don't really know how to say this, but...

However, this should not be used in academic writing. Always finish your sentences!

An ellipsis can also indicate that material has been taken out from a long quote. For example, your original source says:

"NOTE: Older grammar books, written before word processors and personal computers were common, may advise using quotation marks in place of italics for such things as titles of books and magazines, examples, and foreign words."

To capture just the essential information, you could write:

"NOTE: Older grammar books . . . may advise using quotation marks in place of italics for such things as titles of books and magazines. . . ."

Use three dots in the middle of a sentence, and four at the end (the ellipsis plus the regular period that comes at the end of a sentence).

Miscellaneous

Traditionally, writers were asked to use two spaces after sentence-final punctuation (period, question mark, or exclamation point). This rule should always be followed if you are using a typewriter, but is usually optional if you are using a word processor (many word processors automatically delete the extra space).

Older grammar books, written before word processors and personal computers were common, may advise using quotation marks in place of italics for such things as titles of books and magazines, examples, and foreign words. If you are using a word processor, use italics unless you are specifically asked to use a style handbook that forbids it.

OLD: I have no idea what "wayzgoose" means.
            Do you have to read <u>Romeo and Juliet</u> for
            class?

MODERN: I have no idea what *wayzgoose* means.
            Do you have to read *Romeo and Juliet* for
            class?

Appendix A
USING SOURCES

Kinds of Sources

Different kinds of writing call for different kinds of information. Below are some common sources of information that writers use.

You will notice that the entries categorize sources as *primary* and *secondary* types. Primary sources involve first-hand information, such as personal experience, direct quotations, an author's novel, or the results of a survey. Secondary sources are ones in which information from primary sources has been interpreted, condensed, or combined with information from other sources. For example, a person's diary would be a primary source about his or her life, but a biography written about the person would be a secondary source. Likewise, raw survey results are primary material, but a political analyst's article interpreting the results would be a secondary source.

Personal Experience [primary]. This is useful in almost every kind of writing. In personal narratives, of course, it is your main source of information. In academic argumentation papers, use it to illustrate or support points in conjunction with other kinds of information. Since personal experience is difficult to prove, and only gives information about what happened to one individual, it is usually not sufficient on its own.

First-hand Interviews [primary]. These are interviews that you conduct yourself or the transcripts of interviews someone else did. These are useful whenever you want to write about the interviewee's opinions or life experiences or are interested in his or her exact words.

Interview Reports [secondary]. These are descriptions of an interview, usually written by the interviewer, who has made decisions about what to include, what to quote directly, and what to paraphrase. When using interview reports, keep in mind that you are getting the *interviewer's* selective account of the interview, which may be biased.

Survey Results [primary or secondary]. Survey results tell you how people responded to a set of questions or prompts from the survey itself. They are, therefore, useful in any kind of writing about people's attitudes or opinions. There are three important points to keep in mind when using surveys, however:

1. They represent people's *responses*, which may or may not be the truth (even if 98 percent of the public said they thought the moon was made of green cheese, the moon would still be made of rock).

2. People's responses are heavily influenced by how surveys are worded.

3. Most survey results you see in the news have been interpreted in some way (and hence count as secondary sources). In an academic paper, it is considered good practice to let the readers know what the actual survey questions or prompts were. If you are using a survey you designed yourself, include a copy of it as an appendix, along with a summary of the responses.

Texts (e.g. novels, essays) [primary]. You can use a text as a primary source if you are writing about *what is in that text*. If you want to demonstrate that Shakespeare used the word *gleek* to mean "sing," you could cite a line of *A Midsummer Night's Dream* in which he does just that. In other words, if you are writing *about* someone's essay on gun control, the essay itself is a primary source; if you are writing about gun control, the essay is a secondary source.

General Encyclopedias (e.g., World Book, Encarta) [secondary]. Although these are good places to *start* reading about areas with which you are initially unfamiliar, if you are writing an academic paper, you should use them only to find out which kinds of more specific sources you should use. In other words, use them for background reading before you gather information that you will actually use in the paper. In research papers, particularly college papers, citing general encyclopedias makes a bad impression (like showing up to a motorcycle rally with training wheels on your bike).

Specialist Encyclopedias (e.g. The Oxford Companion to Philosophy, The Encyclopedia of Botany) [secondary]. Unlike general encyclopedias, specialist encyclopedias are devoted to particular areas of knowledge are usually considered good scholarly sources for purposes of academic writing.

Magazine and Journal Articles [usually secondary]. Publishers use the terms *magazine* and *journal* interchangeably, but writers and librarians frequently make a distinction between the two. In general, people read magazines because they want to, and the magazine articles are about topics that people want to read about in their spare time. *Time* and *National Geographic* are good examples. People read journals because they need to. Journals are related to their occupations, and whether or not readers enjoy reading them is not particularly relevant. Examples include *Philosophical Quarterly* and *The New England Journal of Medicine*. Thus, magazines frequently have color pictures, which are thought to capture readers' interest, and rarely do magazines feature complex material such as mathematical equations or technical diagrams. Journals, on the other hand, include pictures only when the article cannot be understood without them, and they may devote entire pages to equations, diagrams, tables, or other complicated forms of explanation. As you might expect, journal articles carry more weight in an academic paper than magazine articles do.

Newspaper Articles [primary or secondary]. Since newspapers are written to be read easily by the vast majority of readers, they rarely go into much detail on particular subjects. They are a valuable source of information about current events, politics, and local issues (you are unlikely to find information on your hometown's Rutabaga Festival anywhere else!), but if you are writing about wider issues, you should use newspaper articles only in conjunction with other kinds of sources. For example, if you are writing a paper on global warming, newspaper articles would make good sources *if* you used them along with material from scientific journals.

Nonfiction Books [usually secondary]. Whether or not these make good sources depends on the reputation of the book's author and how up-to-date the information is. A physics text from 1912, for example, would not be a very good source of information on modern physics.

Web Pages [usually secondary]. The important thing to remember about much of the material on the Internet is that people can post almost anything they want. Therefore, whether or not a web page or site is a good source depends on who produced it. If the site is associated with a reputable organization, or the author has documented his or her credentials as an authority on the subject of the site, then it may be useful. However, it is good practice to avoid using Internet sources exclusively; use them to support points you are also supporting with other material.

Documenting Sources

If you are writing a formal academic paper, you will be expected to follow a set of guidelines for documenting sources. There are several of these, since different fields use different formats; for example, English uses the guidelines from the Modern Language Association (MLA) and psychology uses guidelines from the American Psychological Association. The most widely used guide is the comprehensive and detailed book *The Chicago Manual of Style,* published by the University of Chicago Press. However, the different formats typically use the same information—they just organize it differently. Before you worry about how to set up your citation and bibliographic entries, you need to make certain that when you get information from an outside source, you write down the vital facts about it; that way, the information will all be there later when you go about constructing your entries.

Things to write down:

For any publication:

- *Author.* Not all publications have listed authors, but most do, and the name will always be part of the entry for the work.
- *Publication date.* If you are using a source that has been reprinted a number of times, use the most recent date.
- *Title.*
- *Page numbers for any specific information you use.* It is absolutely vital to keep a record of which pages you get information from. For example, if you want to mention in your paper that there are

two major dialects of Albanian, and you read that on page 23 of your source, make sure you note that the fact came from that page. You may need it when you write the paper (after all, that is not exactly common knowledge).

For books:

- *Edition.* You only need list this if you are *not* using a first edition (e.g. second edition).
- *Place of publication.*
- *Publishing company.*
- *Date of publication.*

For article collections or edited volumes

- *The editor(s)' name(s).* Any source that has "edited by" on the front cover, or has what looks like an author's name followed by "ed." (e.g. Mary Smith, ed.) is a collection of material that other people wrote and the editor assembled. You will need the name of the author and title of the section or sections you are using, and the name of the editor and the name of the collection. For example, Sebastian Mitchell may have written an article titled "The Sinking of the *Titanic*" that appears in Mary Smith's edited book titled *Famous Shipwrecks.* You'd need both titles, as well as Mitchell's and Smith's names.

For articles, chapters, or any section of a longer work:

- *The page numbers of the section.* In other words, the starting and ending pages (e.g., 12–48).

For periodicals (journals, magazines, newspapers):

- *The volume and issue numbers.* These will usually appear toward the top of the front cover. Not all newspapers use these, but almost all journals and magazines do.

For Internet web pages:

- *The URL.* This is the full address, as it appears in the address window in the browser you are using (e.g. *http://www.sampleurl.com*).
- *The access date or "Last Modified" date.* If the page lists when it was last modified, use that date; otherwise, write down when you accessed it.

For translations:

- *The translator's name and book information for the translation.* If you are quoting *War and Peace*, by Leo Tolstoy, you are probably not reading it in the original Russian, and you will need the name of the translator as well as the date, place of publication, etc., for the book you are using.

Appendix B
COMMONLY MISUSED WORDS

affect/effect
In normal usage, *affect* is a verb, while *effect* is a noun: *The food **affected** my health, and the bad **effect** lasted for months.* There are other, more specialized uses for the two words, but these are the most common.

among/between
Traditionally, *between* is only used for two objects, while *among* is used for three or more. Of course, famous authors have ignored this repeatedly throughout the past thousand years, but your instructor probably won't.

amount/number
Don't use *amount* for things that are countable—like people, for instance. Saying that *There was a large amount of people in the room* doesn't necessarily mean that there were a lot of people; there could have been only a few extremely large people.

as/like
As implies equivalence, while *like* just implies similarity. *He acted as a judge* means, "For most purposes, he was a judge," while *he acted like a judge* means, "he behaved in ways similar to how a judge would behave."

choose/chose
Choose is present tense, while *chose* is past tense. ***Choose** carefully, or else tomorrow you'll be thinking you **chose** foolishly.*

different from/ different than	Although there are situations where you can use *different than*, it is much safer just to use *different from*. Instructors sometimes get picky about this one.
imminent/ eminent	*Imminent* events are ones that are about to occur any second. *Eminent* people are famous or well-known ones.
imply/infer	These are opposites, in a sense. Words, ideas, or evidence can *imply* something, but only people can *infer* something based on evidence. You can substitute *deduce* for *infer*, and *hint* for *imply*.
insure/ensure	*Insure* is only for insurance policies; *ensure* is roughly equivalent to *make sure*. *His fear of accidents **ensured** that he **insured** his car.*
less/fewer	In formal writing, *fewer* is for things you can count (nouns that take a plural form). *I bought **less** sugar and **fewer** apples.*
lie/lay	This is an intransitive/transitive pair . Use *lay* only as a transitive verb (a verb that requires an object). *It is lying where I laid it yesterday.*
loose/lose	*Loose* is usually an adjective (*loose change*), although there is a rather rare verb spelled the same way that means "release" or "unleash" (*The sheriff threatened to **loose** his dogs on us*). *Lose* (past tense *lost*) is a verb.
really	In formal writing, substitute *very* if you are using it to modify an adjective (e.g., *The movie was very boring* instead of *The movie was really boring*).
site/sight/cite	A *site* is a place; *sight* refers to vision; and *cite* is a verb referring to the act of including a citation (as in *You must cite sources to avoid plagiarism*).

sit/set	Another intransitive/transitive pair. You **sit** in a chair, but you **set** something in the chair.
there/their they're	*They're* can only be used as the contraction for *they are*, while *there* is the possessive form of *they*. *There* is a place term. ***They're** upset that they left **their** keys **there**.*
to/too/two	*Two* is a number, *to* is a preposition, and *too* is a qualifier or adverb. ***Two** of them went **to** Cancun **too**, but found it **too** hot.*

One Word or Two?

already/all ready	*All ready* can be paraphrased as "completely ready" or "all (of us were) ready." Use *already* otherwise. *We were **all ready** to meet, but discovered that they had **already** left.*
anyone/any one	*Anyone* can only be used for people, while *any one* can refer to any single object, idea, person, etc.
awhile/a while	*Awhile* is used with verbs, and for some strange reason denotes a shorter time period than *a while* does. *A while* is a noun phrase, and is frequently used after prepositions.
everyday/every day	You can substitute *normal* or *usual* for *everyday*; you can substitute *on each day* or *daily* for *every day*. *Since I work at home, I can wear **everyday** clothes **every day**.*
everyone/every one	*Everyone* refers only to people, while *every one* refers to "every single object, person, idea, etc."

Never Use These!

alot	It should always be two words.
alright	Make it two words (*all right*)
should of	Also avoid *could of*, *might of*, etc. The correct form is *should have*.

Appendix C
QUICK OVERVIEW FOR COMMAS AND QUOTES

Commas

General Patterns

> **introducer, Sentence.**
>> *Fortunately, the bomb did not explode.*
>
> **Subject, interrupter, Predicate.**
>> *The rabbit, to my surprise, looked sick.*
>
> **Sentence, ender.**
>> *The supervisor was unimpressed, however.*

Clause-Combining Patterns

> **[Independent clause], <u>conjunction</u> [Independent Clause].**
>> *[We ordered sandwiches], <u>and</u> [they bought bagels].*
>
> **[Independent Clause]; [Independent Clause].**
>> *[We ordered sandwiches]; [they bought bagels].*

[Independent Clause] [Dependent Clause].
[The travelers departed][although they needed rest].

[Dependent Clause], [Independent Clause].
[Although they needed rest],[the travelers departed].

[Independent Clause]; connective, [Independent Clause]
[We ordered sandwiches]; however,[they bought bagels].

Direct Quotations

Statement, "Statement."
He said, "There's a bear in the back yard."

Statement, "Question?"
He asked, "Is there a bear in the back yard?"

Statement, "Exclamation!"
He shouted, "There's a bear in the back yard!"

Question, "Statement"?
Did I just hear him say, "There's a bear in the back yard"?

Question, "Question?"?
Did I just hear him say, "Is there a bear in the yard?"?

Exclamation, "Question?"!
I just heard him ask, "Is that a bomb?"!

Index